I Got In!

The Ultimate College Audition Guide for Acting and Musical Theater

Mary Anna Dennard

Website design by Brooks Dennard
www.brooksdennard.com

All photography by Kelsey Edwards
www.kelseyedwardsphoto.com

Book cover design and concept by
David Dennard, Kelsey Edwards, and Suzee Benjamin

Acknowledgments

Special thanks to the students on my cover, my husband David, my sister Suzee, Nancy "Normal" Marston and Karen Kohlhaas for their guidance, and to all the wonderful college auditors who contributed quotes.

I regard the theater as the greatest of all art forms, the most immediate way in which a human being can share with another the sense of what it means to be human.

—Oscar Wilde

I dedicate this book to my students.

You are my children and have enriched my life beyond measure.

I love you.

xxx, Moo

My students have been accepted into a wide variety of acting and musical theater programs including the following: Baldwin-Wallace College, Boston Conservatory, Boston University, California Institute for the Arts, Carnegie Mellon University, Chapman College, Cincinnati Conservatory of Music, Elon University, Emerson College, Indiana University, Ithaca College, Marymount Manhattan College, University of Michigan, Milikin College, North Carolina School of The Arts, New York University's Tisch School of the Arts, New York University/ Steinhardt, Ohio Northern University, University of Oklahoma, Oklahoma City University, Otterbein College, Pace University, Pennsylvania State University, Point Park University, Roosevelt University, Shenandoah Conservatory, Southern Methodist University, Syracuse University, University of Oklahoma, University of Miami, University of the Arts, University of Southern California, Viterbo University, and Webster University.

National Foundation for Advancement in the Arts Awards include; Presidential Scholars, Finalists, Honorable Mention, and Merit Award Winners.

National Shakespeare Competition Winner.

About the Author

Mary Anna Dennard received her training at The American Conservatory Theater in San Francisco. She began working as a casting director and acting coach in Los Angeles in 1980. Her fifteen years of casting credits have garnered Clios, Emmys, Academy Awards, and a Peabody Award.

Since 2000, she has been a college audition coach for programs in acting and musical theater and has been dubbed "The Princeton Review for Theater Auditions." As a nationally recognized expert in her field, Mary Anna has coached hundreds of students from all over the country, who have been accepted into the most prestigious college training programs in the United States and Europe. Her former students have gone on to have successful careers after college in the recording industry, on television, in motion pictures, and on Broadway. Mary Anna is a special contributor to the New York Times Theatre Section's Artsbeat blog, and a frequent master teacher and guest speaker.

Visit her Web site, www.collegeauditioncoach.com.

Contents

Introduction

This book is meant to serve as a guide for students and parents. I hope you find it helpful as you prepare for your college audition in acting or musical theater. The skill required to become a performing artist is a craft that must be learned. College is an opportune place for you to receive your training, and there is a wide variety of excellent institutions from which to choose.

Included in this book is information based on the decade that I have been successfully coaching students for this very specialized and highly competitive audition. My recommendations are based on my subjective opinions, much like the audition process itself.

Many factors come into play when colleges and universities are evaluating your potential, but none carry more weight than the audition itself. Many schools tell me it counts for 80 percent.

Each year I check in with dozens of college auditors to find out what they are looking for so that my guidance is current and up-to-date. I am proud to say that my students have met with great success. If you follow the advice I have laid out, you will have success too.

In the middle of writing this book, my husband and I went to an exhibit at the Dallas Museum of Art entitled "All The World's A Stage: Celebrating Performance in the Visual Arts." This well-known Oscar Wilde quote was included in the exhibit: "I regard the theater as the greatest of all art forms, the most immediate way in which a human being can share with another the sense of what it means to be human."

As you read this handbook, remember the deeper meaning of why we feel called to be artists. Training is only one part of your journey of discovery. The rest of your process has as much to do with the human connection as it does with the expression of your artistry. The re-creation of human behavior on stage begins with the human connection off stage. As artists we are all lovers and examiners of humankind. Remember the love, the joy, and the inspiration that calls you to share your gifts.

Chapter 1

Getting Started

This Is a Competition

Imagine your world to be the size of a circle that would fit into the palm of your hand. As you enter the college audition process, your palm-sized world is about to explode. It is going to get huge. All of a sudden you are going to be competing on a national scale, possibly for the first time in your life. Within that palm-sized circumference, you might have been the star of your high school theater program, had the lead in the musicals, landed the plum roles in the plays, or been elected the president of thespians. In this new expanded sphere, every star of every musical theater and drama program in every high school in the United States is vying for the same few select openings at these colleges. You are now competing against all of them in the national arena. College auditors are going to be auditioning other students from around the country, possibly the world, and the pallet from which they choose will be a global pallet.

The most elite schools accept fewer than 5 percent of the students who audition. Schools considered somewhat less selective accept fewer than 15 percent. With these odds you might sooner win your state lottery than get into one of these highly selective programs! To make the margin even more competitive, colleges have reported a substantial increase in applicants for acting and musical theater over the last three years. Brent Wagner, chair of the Department of Musical Theatre at the University of Michigan, recently told me that his applicants were up 20 percent in a single year. Even in light of our nation's economic challenges, the college representatives whom I speak with acknowledge the increase in applicants for acting and musical theater programs. This popularity might be explained by our fascination with YouTube, *American Idol,* and *Glee.* Whatever the reason, it is a trend that seems to be on the rise. This creates a highly competitive admission process. Therefore, anything you can do to broaden your world, to broaden your scope, to open up the little circle that fits inside the palm of your hand will enable you to compete more successfully.

In this book I give you the tools you need to be the most competitive and yield the best results. I tell you how to compete on a national scale and how to expand your world of knowledge. I share the trade secrets I have developed over the years of successfully coaching hundreds of students through the college audition process. If you follow my instructions, you will be completely and thoroughly prepared for your college audition.

Use Your Summer

My first piece of advice is to get started on this process your junior year. The summer after your junior year will be your last opportunity to take training to advance your skills and add an impressive credit to your resume. There are many wonderful precollege programs in acting and musical theater as well as some wonderful summer training camps. I provide you a list of the ones I recommend under "Resources" at the end of the book.

There are two kinds of summer training offerings. One is the precollege experience; the other is a summer performing arts camp. The advantage of a precollege summer program is the opportunity to be on a real college campus, live in a dormitory, experience a little bit of college life, and receive instruction from college and university faculty.

Sometimes college credit is offered. A summer training camp allows you to gain more experience, provides an opportunity to hone your skills, furthers your training in acting or musical theater, and enables you to make new friends who are also interested in performing. Some summer training culminates in a production. However, some do not. So if gaining another performance credit is important to you, you need to research which camps perform full productions and which ones simply present scenes or a cabaret-styled show. Some of the summer programs last only a week, perfect if you are trying to fit in a brief course of study in between summer jobs or family vacations. Other programs will take up the majority of your summer, lasting up to eight weeks. Some of these programs require an audition; some do not. You will have to look into the individual programs to see which require an audition and what those requirements are. Audition procedures can vary from DVD audition submissions to on-campus auditions. Some programs travel to various cities to conduct regional auditions. The audition circuit for the summer programs usually begins in December or January.

Many of the offerings can be pricey, so If the summer training program is not an option for you, I advise you to take part in whatever summer performance opportunities are available for you in your hometown through a community theater, church, temple, internship, or local arts camp.

Use this time wisely because it will be your final opportunity to get advanced experience, get a credit for your resume, and meet performers from outside your local community. It will be one of the last opportunities to expand your palm-sized world before the real college competition begins.

College Visits

I advise against scheduling college visits too early. Visiting colleges is expensive, time consuming, and stressful. Students have to take time away from their studies and school activities. Parents have to take off from work. And these days air travel is no fun. You can become smitten with one school during a visit and mentally shut the door on other wonderful schools. Furthermore, it is not feasible to visit every school if you have the typical list of ten to fifteen schools. Remember, you may be admitted into only three or four schools on your list. To have spent all that time and money visiting colleges that you are not admitted to seems wasteful.

Many helpful tools for evaluating college performing arts training programs do not involve getting on an airplane. Explore virtual tours on college Web sites, attend college performing arts fairs, e-mail college admissions advisers, and Facebook current students to begin a dialogue. Families can connect in a very personal way with these colleges without visiting the actual campus. I have a free podcast series on my Web site that is an excellent source for information. In the podcasts I interview` theater and musical theater department heads of various colleges. These interviews contain valuable firsthand advice about the audition process, admissions, and training that the schools offer. Go to my Web site, www.collegeauditioncoach.com, click on "Podcasts" on the menu bar.

When should you visit? Wait until you see which schools you gain admission to and then visit those schools with your parents. When you visit after you have been accepted, it is a much different visit. You know the school wants you and that this school is a real possibility for you. You will audit a class, see a production, stay in a dorm, and eat in the commissary. Your parents can visit the financial aid office and present any scholarship offers from other schools for comparison. Then after visiting, you can make a clear and well-informed final decision.

Chapter 2

Compiling Your College List

Helpful Resources

Whether you are a rising senior or in your senior year, the first thing you need to do is compile your college list. A great way to begin your list is to attend the National Association For College Admissions Counseling (NACAC) Performing Arts College Fair. NACAC has a performing arts and visual arts college fair that travels to seventeen cities throughout the United States beginning in the fall. The fair is free and an excellent way to meet with college representatives from the theater and musical theater university programs. There are as many as eighty colleges that participate in the NACAC Performing Arts College Fair. You can find their Web site address under "Resources" at the end of the book.

Most traditional college fairs include representatives from the college's general admissions office, and they know little about the theater programs. The NACAC Performing Arts College Fair is different because the representatives are experts in their college's theater admissions process and can answer most any questions you have. You can learn about educational opportunities, admission and financial aid, audition and entrance requirements, and much more by meeting with representatives from colleges, universities, conservatories, festivals, and other educational institutions with specialized programs in the visual arts and performing arts.

It is a good idea for parents and students to attend together. Go with an organized list of schools that interest you. Write down questions for the colleges, and take detailed notes. The NACAC Performing Arts College Fair is usually crowded and can be somewhat overwhelming. But if you are well organized, it can be a very productive information-gathering session. It will definitely aid you in focusing your college list. It is best if you attend your junior year, but if you are already a senior, you can still go to NACAC in the fall and get a lot accomplished.

There is a wonderful Web site resource called *Schools for Theatre*, and I also give you that Web site address under "Resources" at the end of the book. The site bills itself as the only comprehensive online guide to theater schools and universities that offer programs in theater arts. Using the search engine, prospective students can find schools that offer programs in acting, musical theater, directing, design, technical theater, stage management, theater management, theater education, theater for youth, history and criticism, playwriting, and drama therapy. Detailed information on each school includes audition deadlines, alumni and faculty lists, and curriculum. You can search by desired major or by name of college and find wonderful direct links to the college theater's audition page. It is a quick and easy way to go directly to the Web site and find information about a college's audition requirements without having to crawl your way through the often confusing college and university Web sites.

Your high school's college counselor should be able to help you compile your list although she or he may not have specific knowledge about theater and musical theater programs. You can still work together to start gathering lists of colleges. Your school counselor has some general knowledge that is helpful in terms of schools that would be a good academic fit for you (taking into consideration your GPA, SAT, and ACT scores) and nonaudition schools. You also want to keep your ears and eyes open for any friends who are performers and attending college BFA and BA programs in acting and musical theater. However,

I want to caution you that a school that is a perfect fit for your best friend may not be the right school for you.

If you are in a financial position to hire an independent college counselor, I recommend Susan Taub and Erin Ogren. Susan has thoroughly researched statistics for performing arts colleges and is familiar with the admission process, various degree programs, and curriculum, especially in acting and musical theater. Erin Ogren of Central Coast College Consultants has a special Performing Arts Package for acting and musical theatre applicants. Erin has advanced college counseling accreditation and has been through the process with her own child recently, so she knows the ropes. I give both of their contact information under "Resources."

Your public library is a free resource where you can find guidebooks that might be helpful. You can find many helpful reference books in bookstores, books such as *Guide for Performing Arts Majors* by Peterson's.

A free college-bound Internet community source is a Web site called *College Confidential*, also known as CC. CC has theater and musical theater chat rooms where laypersons, students, and family members who are going through the college audition process share advice, experiences, and opinions. However, to get accurate and up-to-date information, you always need to direct your inquiries to the individual colleges. I have listed CC's Web address under "Resources" at the end of the book.

If you like to network and want a free option for connecting to current college performing arts students, try Facebook. As a relatively new tool, I have found Facebook extremely helpful with my private students. My current students friend my former students who are attending colleges and universities that are of interest to them. Many students (current and prospective) create groups where they can trade information about various performing arts programs. As Facebook friends, students can share information from firsthand experiences that they are not likely to get from college recruitment representatives. Often the best way to get personal and up-to-date information is to talk to a student who is currently enrolled in one of those programs that you are interested in. I caution you again that what is best for one person may not be what is best for you.

It is important for you to keep an open mind and think about the specific things that you want in a college and the kind of training you need. Do you want to live in a certain part of the country? Do you want a school that has strong academics? Do you want the full college experience with football, Greek life, and student government? Do you want a conservatory? Do you want to be close to home? Do you want to be far away from home? Is tuition going to be a make-or-break factor in your decision? What kinds of scholarships are available? All these things are important considerations. Your college experience not only will be about your training in acting or musical theater but also will have a lasting impact on you in other ways. You may take up residence in the town where you go to college, make lifelong friends or meet the love of your life. You need to think about the kinds of people you want to go to school with and the environment in which you will be living. The college experience will enrich your life in ways beyond your training. These considerations are all part of the process. This information-gathering expedition is just one more way to expand your world.

Performing Arts Degrees

It is important that you know what kind of degree you want. So let us explore the different degrees that are available for the study of acting and musical theater. The degrees that are going to be of greatest interest to you are a bachelor of arts (BA), a bachelor of fine arts,

(BFA), and, to a lesser degree, a bachelor of music (BM). You could also consider a conservatory, which would include the BFA degree. A handful of training schools offer an eighteen-month or two-year associate of applied arts degree program. KD Studio in Dallas and The Neighborhood Playhouse and Circle in The Square in New York City are examples. However, with the AA accreditation you will not graduate with a college degree, only a certificate.

BA, BFA, BM, Conservatory

A BA is a degree that is commonly defined as 30 percent to 40 percent curriculum in your major, with the remainder in general education and electives. If you want to double major or minor in something or maybe study abroad, a BA is an excellent degree plan for you. The BA is traditionally seen as a degree for people who have a wide variety of interests besides acting, singing, and dancing.

The BFA is defined as 60 percent to 80 percent curriculum in your major, with the remainder in general education and electives. The BFA leaves little room for a minor that is substantial, and it would be difficult to double major and still graduate in four years. The BFA curriculum is very intense and does not allow for time during the school year to study abroad; however, you could study abroad in the summer.

With the conservatory-styled BFA degree, expect 80 percent to 95 percent of the courses in your major and very little curriculum in general education. Your course selection is almost entirely related to your major with few or no classes outside your major. And, of course, the student body is going to be made up solely of students who are studying performing degrees. Some colleges, however, offer an intense conservatory style of training in a liberal arts university setting.

Lastly, a BM in musical theater is housed in the school of music and heavily weighted in music theory and classically based music repertoire such as sung through musicals and operettas. This is as opposed to post-1960-styled traditional acting, singing, and dancing musicals. These degrees are fewer in number.

Sometimes it is a good idea to have a mixture of degrees on your college list. But if you think of yourself as a performer first and want to train for the stage through a rigorous, challenging, demanding curriculum that is very performance driven, then head for a BFA. If you have a wide variety of interests and passions in addition to performing and want to explore those studies or want an abroad experience, take the BA route. Many excellent BA programs have a rigorous theater curriculum.

Frankly, directors are split on what kind of actors they like to hire. Some directors prefer actors who have a BA degree because they are well rounded in their education. For example, if you were cast in a production of *Les Miserables* and you had studied the French Revolution, French language, and history, you would make a larger contribution to the rehearsal process. You would bring more to the table, as they say. Whereas a BFA performer might have spent years studying dance, voice, and acting but have little knowledge about French history or French language. On the other hand, one school of thought says that the BFA-trained actor is ready to perform professionally because of the four years of intense performance training.

Whatever the degree, you need to do some real soul searching about what kind of education you want for yourself. Ask yourself these questions: Are your friends at school from other walks of life? Do you have friends who are athletes? Do you have friends who are involved in student government? Do you have friends who are cheerleaders? Or are all your friends actors, dancers, and musical theater types? Chances are if you are used to being around challenging academics and people who have a variety of interests and you go to a conservatory, you may feel like a fish out of water. You may find that your fellow conservatory students are nothing like you. Then again you may welcome that difference. These are all considerations that you need to discuss with your parents.

Reaches, Fits, and Safeties

You may have heard the term *reaches, fits, and safeties* What does that mean? A *reach* is a school that has a very low acceptance rate (under 10 percent), is highly selective, and you dream of attending. A *fit* is a school that—considering your skill set, your type, and the school's acceptance rate—you will have a fairly good chance of being accepted into. A *safety* is a school that does not require an audition and one that you and your high school college counselor are certain you will get into based on your GPA, ACT, and SAT scores.

There are plenty of excellent nonaudition safeties for you to consider. Be sure your safeties have strong, reputable theater departments where you earnestly feel you could be happy if you are rejected from all your audition schools. No one wants to think about that scenario, but you must have a safety net, just in case.

Smart List

I talk a lot with my students about creating a smart list. A smart list is a college list that includes a thoughtful combination of reaches, fits, and safeties. This is essential to your success. Creating a list of colleges is a long process, and your list will evolve over time. The important thing is for you to get the process started. Begin a dialogue with your parents. Begin a dialogue with the universities. Go to the college fairs. Talk to your college counselor. Talk to your performer friends who are already in college. Just get the process started, and do not expect that you are going to have all the answers right away. Know that this list of colleges is going to drive the rest of the process because each school has different audition requirements. And it is important for you to recognize your list as a first step in preparing for the rest of the process. Keep an open mind.

Students often ask how many schools should be on their list. The competition is stiff. You want to be able to have a couple of choices at the end of the day so that you feel as though you have some options. Having talent is not always enough to gain admittance. More often it is about type, not talent. Some colleges may already have someone your type, or they might be actively seeking a type different from yours. I tell this true story of a very talented female student whose type could be classified as brassy, belty, and brunette. She was rejected from her top choice school. When I asked the head of the department for feedback, he told me that she was the most talented girl they had auditioned that day, but they didn't need her type. The school was graduating three petite blonde legit sopranos, and their priority that audition year was to fill the holes in their department. Any other year she probably would have been accepted.

The most competitive category (in term of types auditioning) is the white female category. There are a disproportionately large number of white females auditioning for schools, so there is more competition within that group. For those I recommend a list of ten to fifteen audition schools. If you are an ethnic minority or a male, eight to ten audition schools should be enough. Remember, this does not include nonaudition safety schools. I recommend two safeties for everyone.

The makeup of your college list is more important than the number of schools is. Your smart list should have an equal number of reaches and fits that might include a combination of BAs, BFAs, maybe a BM or conservatory, plus the two nonaudition safeties. Broaden your list and broaden your options.

Chapter 3

Audition Components

Each audition has different components for acting and musical theater. You must check with the individual colleges to find out their requirements. You can find these on the colleges' Web sites. Most acting programs require two monologues. Most musical theater programs require one or two monologues and two songs. A dance combination will likely be a part of the musical theater audition process and sometimes a music theory test. A personal interview is a component of the audition for both acting and musical theater.

Monologues

Most schools require either one or two contemporary monologues. However, many colleges request one contemporary monologue and one classical monologue. This is especially true of straight acting programs. A contemporary monologue is a monologue written from 1900 to present day. A classical monologue is traditionally considered a monologue written before 1900. That would include the Greeks, Shakespeare, Moliere, Calderon, and other pieces written in verse. Although contemporary monologues are written from 1900 to present day, I think it is important to pick monologues written in the last three to ten years. Plays that were written in the 1960s, '70s, and '80s may be overdone and somewhat dated and not the strongest choice.

Colleges require a classical monologue because they want to see (and hear) how you handle verse. In that case Shakespeare is an obvious option. I also like to use modern translations of classical texts because the words are easier to act and easier to speak. (I especially recommend the Richard Wilbur translations of Moliere's works, as well as modern translations by Christopher Hampton and Robert Burstein of other classical works). Translated classical texts can be a refreshing change for the auditors as a nice alternative to Shakespeare. Because Moliere, for example, wrote in rhyming couplets and iambic pentameter, you fulfill the verse requirement and give the auditors something fresh.

Steer clear of any accents or dialects when performing your college monologues. Because the auditors want to get to know who *you* are, it is a hindrance to hide behind a dialect or an accent. It is also important to choose material close to your own personality with an understanding of how you will be cast. Avoid extreme characters. My years as a casting director give me a unique ability to ascertain how to market my students and how colleges will cast you. It is important that you begin to understand this about yourself so you can find appropriate material. Read the *Audition Tips from College Auditors* in the "Resources" section at the end of the book.

I was having a breakfast meeting with the head of one of the most selective college musical theater programs, and we were discussing how students often make the mistake of choosing material outside their castable type. We agreed that this occurs not only in monologues but also in songs choices. Students often sing outside their vocal range and ability. This makes it difficult to ascertain exactly what it is that an actor can do well. But it is possible to show range in your two contrasting monologues and songs without going outside your type. Simply showing contrasting tones and styles is sufficient. The most common mistake young actors make is trying to show too much during an audition. The time limits prohibit you from demonstrating all that you can do in a single audition. With monologues it is always better to show two varying tones within your type: one could be tender and vulnerable and the other could be combative and strong. I cannot stress enough how important it is to stay within your type.

To further assist you in finding appropriate material, some of the college Web sites offer a list of recommended monologues (and a list of monologues to avoid).

Lesser-known works by playwrights of distinction can be a great source for monologue material. I often research well-known classic playwrights—such as Arthur Miller, Tennessee Williams, Eugene O'Neill, Clifford Odets, and William Inge—and find that some of their earlier, more obscure works or one-acts have hidden monologue treasures.

Avoid monologues written specifically for monologue books. Your college audition monologues need to be from significant playwrights: either important young, contemporary writers or established produced writers. A wonderful resource for cutting-edge writers of new works is New Dramatists (ND) in New York. ND was founded in 1949 to support and develop playwrights. Their Web site is listed under "Resources." If you contact them via e-mail or phone, they are helpful about photocopying scripts of their writers (usually in manuscript form) and mailing them to you for a nominal fee. There is information about ND member playwrights and descriptions of their plays on the Web site. ND is an excellent place to discover young,` new writers whose works are being commissioned and performed at some of the most important regional theaters in the country and off Broadway.

The National Foundation for the Advancement of the Arts also lists the winning monologues from their annual Young Arts competition on their Web site. You might also go to some of the country's leading regional theaters' Web sites to see what plays they are producing, as well as the individual college Web sites for their performance season listing of shows. You need to be reading *Playbill* and the *New York Times* "Theater" section regularly to keep up with current productions and writers. The "Resources" section has these Web sites. And *go to the theater*. Expand your knowledge of plays, playwrights, and composers. It is part of expanding your world. I go into detail about how I choose monologues and the importance of the well-chosen monologue in Chapter 7, "Choosing Monologue Material,"

Time Limits

When reading the college Web sites regarding monologue requirements, pay close attention to the time limits and adhere to them. Increasingly, musical theater auditions are requesting a maximum of no more than one minute for the monologue. Straight acting programs tend to have longer time limits. Usually ninety seconds to two minutes for each monologue or a combined time not to exceed five minutes. Most colleges do not time your monologues, but some actually do. Pay special attention to the time, and rehearse with a stopwatch for accuracy. Time limits are strictly enforced in some situations, like consortium auditions, state thespian conventions, and showcases to keep things running on time.

I always recommend having extra monologues because the auditors will often ask, "Do you have something else?" You want to be able to respond, "Why, yes, I do." If you are asked for additional monologues, the time limit is going to be less of an issue. By asking for additional monologues, the auditors indicate that they are interested in spending more time with you.

Songs

For musical theater auditions (and for a very few acting auditions), you will be required to sing in addition to presenting your one or two monologues. Acting programs that require you to sing usually accept one song of your choosing, sung a cappella. For musical theater auditions, colleges want to hear two songs: an up-tempo song and a ballad. Up-tempo is just that, an upbeat, lively tune. A ballad is slower and contains a legato line or sustained vocal line. Even when schools do not require it, have one song that was written before 1960. Some schools (those more classically based or those offering a BM) require an art song or classical song sung in a foreign language. And some schools are now requesting one pop/rock song in addition to a standard musical theatre song. Please check with the colleges to be sure you are clear about their song requirements.

For musical theater programs, singing is the first and foremost component. Establishing your vocal identity is important. A college will not admit a student in a musical theater program who does not have a strong voice or show potential for a strong voice. You can be the best actor in the world, but if your singing is not up to par, a musical theater program will not accept you.

Choosing the correct song to showcase your vocal strengths for your castable type is extremely important. Acting the song is another crucial component for song preparation, and your college auditors look specifically for your understanding of this important component.

Song Cuttings

Songs will need to be in the correct key with cuttings that make sense musically and still tell the story. When colleges conduct off-campus auditions, they may not provide live accompaniment. This will require you to prepare your music on recorded tracks. Simple recorded piano accompaniment is appropriate. Never use karaoke tracks.

Sixteen-bar and Thirty-two–bar cuttings are the standard requested from the schools. You will need those cuttings in piano and vocal sheet-music form. In addition, you will need recorded piano for both sixteen-bar and thirty-two–bar cuttings for those auditions using tracks. Of course, you need to have the full versions of your songs, but know that the sixteen-bar and thirty-two–bar cuttings are the ones that colleges ask for. Additionally, you need to have your songbook ready. Your "book" should contain other musical theater and pop repertoire that you are familiar with in case the auditors ask you to sing additional material.

Recorded Tracks

When you prepare your recorded tracks, you will need to bring playback equipment with you. This is your responsibility; the school will not provide it. If you are using your iPod for playback, be sure that you have a battery-operated deck with speakers so you do not have to worry about finding an electrical outlet. IPod users might want to create a play list for each school with appropriate cuttings for each song.

If you are using a CD player, use batteries so that you can easily get to your playback. Be sure that you have the right cuttings of your songs in the correct order. An important note: be sure the disk plays in your portable player. If you have burned it on your home computer and have listened to it only on your home computer or in your car, there is a chance it may not play on your portable CD player. These CDs can be quirky. Thorough preparation will ensure that you do not have any surprises when you get in the room with the auditors. Rehearse with your playback equipment and the volume levels. And have fresh batteries on hand!

Working with Your Accompanist

You will likely not know the caliber of your accompanist, so choose your music wisely. Many composers (for example, Jason Robert Brown, Adam Guettel, and Stephen Sondheim) are difficult to play, especially if the accompanist has never seen their music.

Take the lead when you are singing. If the tempo is not to your liking, do not glare at the accompanist. Push or pull the accompanist toward your tempo. Your auditors are probably aware, from other people having similar difficulties, that the problem is not you.

If a pianist is flubbing, do not keep looking toward the piano. Take the lead by physically turning the *other* way. Keep the attention and focus on your singing.

Usually, accompanists do the best they can. Even if the entire process is a train wreck, maintain your poise and professionalism. That will be noted. Also, *always* thank the accompanist by name.

Prep Your Music

Never hand an accompanist a stack of single-sided copies. The best solution is to have your book of rep (short for repertoire). This is a narrow three-ring binder containing your sheet music. The sheets should be loaded double-sided in nonglare sheet protectors. Or you can use double-sided copies. Even in the notebook, do not put in single-sided copies. Think about it; every time a pianist turns a page, he or she has to take a hand off the piano for a time. Go through your music and make sure none of the pages stick to each other. Be sure the name of the song is written at the top of each page. Do not hand the accompanist a copy of music with chord symbols written above the music, even if you plan on doing it in the original key.

If you are doing a rubato, tenuto, or fermata, make sure it is marked in the music; highlight it instead of just verbally calling attention to it. Anything you tell your accompanist should already be marked in the music.

It is unlikely to happen in a short cut, but if there is a repeat (marked by a DS or DC), make sure it is clearly marked. If it is more than a page back, put a sticky flag or a paper clip on the top of the page it is going back to. Or to make things easier, just make a second copy of the page to be repeated and attach it after the DS or DC. That way the accompanist has to worry about reading music in only one direction.

If you make a cut that is longer than a few measures (which can be marked in red or something very obvious), see if the layout of the song makes sense to physically cut and paste the music. Then make a clean copy of that. You do not want the accompanist fumbling through an unnecessary page turn to find it.

Setting Your Tempo

As you approach the piano, introduce yourself and be sure to get the accompanist's name. Then set the tempo. Take your time to do this, but do not take too long. You should be able to communicate this in about thirty seconds or less. Do not take minutes. Never tap out the rhythm for the accompanist. Just sing a couple of measures at the desired tempo. And *never* ask an accompanist to transpose for you.

Your Book of Rep

Your book is your binder with your repertoire in it. In the rep book, you should have the cut version and a copy of the whole song, in case the auditor asks to hear more. If you have sixteen-bar and thirty-two–bar cuts of the same song, have separate copies of them so the accompanist is not wondering at which "stop here" to stop. In addition to your audition songs, your book of rep should contain other songs you have performed or know well, in case you are asked to sing additional material. Take note: a fully prepared college audition book of song repertoire contains 4-6 contrasting musical theatre songs that contrasting vocally, musically, in era of composition, and castable type. And if you have solid classical training, you might want to include an aria. If you have a pop/rock song that shows off your vocal strength, you should include that as well.

Dance Combination

For musical theater college auditions, there is almost always a required dance element. This consists of a musical theater dance combination, typically four 8-counts of music. A member of the faculty teaches the combo in a group setting. You will have approximately fifteen to 30 minutes to learn the combination. This component is an important element of the audition requirement and is something you should be training for in the years and months leading up to the audition. You are going to have to be ready to execute ably whatever combination is thrown at you. On campus the audition usually takes place in a university dance studio. If the audition is off campus, for example at the Chicago Unified site, dancers perform in a hotel meeting room on a carpeted floor with no mirrors.

The combinations may include barre work, across the floor, and then four 8-counts of a musical theater style combination. Tap dancing is not typically part of any of the college dance combinations. These combinations are taught quickly and include various degrees of difficulty, which differ from school to school. There may be an opportunity for a few counts of dance improvisation. College dance combos are ballet based. To prepare, start as soon as you can and get in a ballet class. Ballet is to dance what Latin is to language.

It is your foundation. You should be dancing at least three times a week, learning the ballet terminology, and building your confidence so that you bring character to the combination and look as though you are having fun. A happy, engaged face can hide a multitude of weaknesses. However, the stronger your dance, the more competitive your overall audition will be. Get in some dance classes and expand you world of knowledge.

Prepared Dance Demonstration

If there is no formal dance combination as part of the audition, you may be asked to demonstrate your dance ability with some movement. I suggest some basic ballet turns; piquée, chaînés, and pirouettes. If you can land a clean double, by all means show that. Show your extension with a developpe or penche. If you are more advanced, show a grande jete and some fouettés. Many schools welcome a prechoreographed dance combination under one minute long for more advanced dancers. If you choose that option, be sure you have your recorded music cued up and ready. This is permissible only if there is no formal dance combination given at the audition.

Music Theory Test

Some musical theater auditions will ask you to take a music theory test. Sometimes this is a test on a piece of paper or a sight-reading exercise that you do with the accompanist and the auditor. Sometimes it is a test that you take by playing the piano. It varies with each school. If there is a theory test, ask questions of the college before the audition about what kind of test it is and how it is going to be administered. Schools are interested to know if you play a musical instrument and if you compose music. Usually the music theory test is used for placement and is not an admission qualifier.

The Adjustment

Another creative and impromptu part of the audition is what is called "an adjustment." You may or may not be called upon to perform an adjustment. If you are, I want you to know what to expect. The auditors may ask you to perform your monologue or song again with a new direction, objective, or tone. The reason for an adjustment is for the auditors to see how flexible, malleable, and creative you are. Also, this can tell them how well you think on your feet and how well you take direction. It is unlikely that they are displeased with your direction, but more likely that they are interested in you and want to see more. Barbara Mackenzie-Wood, Head of Acting/Musical Theatre at the School of Drama at Carnegie Mellon University, told me, "When I audition them, I will often ask them to do it in a different way. Not that I don't like what they've done with it, but to see how flexible they are." The adjustment can be the most enjoyable part of the audition and an experience that really makes you feel like an actor.

Be ready for anything. One of the most selective schools has been known to ask students to perform their monologue like a chicken or run around the room and scream or do it with a southern accent. Sometimes auditors might unexpectedly ask you to sing a song from one of the shows on your resume. They may ask you to sing something else from your book of rep. During the dance portion of the audition, they may ask you to improvise some kind of movement. Do not let these things throw you. Expect anything and be prepared for everything. The important thing for you to do is to take their direction with ease and complete commitment and have fun with it.

Audition Feedback

As a rule, college auditors do not give you any indication about your chances of admission or feedback about how you performed.

Decisions about acceptance, rejection, deferral, and waitlist come later in an official form. Most decisions come via snail mail although I have more and more students hearing through e-mail and phone calls (acceptances only). You will probably not know what kind of impression you have made on the auditors after your audition. It is best not to try to second-guess what they are thinking because you could be very wrong. I had a student at Unifieds come up to me crying after her Carnegie Mellon University audition because she was just sure that it had not gone well at all. She felt she had not given the auditors what they wanted and had disappointed them, herself, and me. I tried to calm her down and reassure her. I advised that she not carry that negative imprint into the next day's auditions. Well, her perceptions could not have been more wrong. She was accepted into the CMU program! They loved her audition and told me how impressed they were with her talents.

So refrain from reading anything into the auditors' reactions because you *never* know what they are thinking. I discuss more on this topic in Chapter 11 when I introduce you to mental management.

Chapter 4

The Personal interview

The Interview Itself

In addition to the performance components, you will most likely be given a personal interview. Sometimes the interviews are very formal and last five to ten minutes. They may take place separately from the rest of the audition, and a separate person or panel might interview you. Sometimes the interview is as brief as just a couple of questions asked to you by the auditors right after you finish your songs or monologues. Sometimes the interview is actually happening without your knowing it. Auditors from one of the more prestigious colleges revealed to me that the interview is actually secretly conducted during the teaching of the dance combination. Other college auditors have told me that they actually interview candidates while they are in the waiting room, before their audition. But as Tommy Newton, the director of recruitment at Southern Methodist University's Meadows School of the Arts, so astutely points out, your audition actually begins the minute you make that first phone call and send that first e-mail to the college.

The purpose of the interview is for the college auditors to have an opportunity to get to know you as a person. What can they learn about you aside from your resume, essay, head shot, monologues, and songs? Do they like you? Are you articulate? Do they think you are smart? Do you have a good work ethic? Are you the kind of student they would like to spend four years with? What other kinds of interests do you have? These are the things that can be gleamed from an interview.

A lot of students overlook the interview. It is something they just do not add to the equation. I feel, however, that it is extremely important and could be the difference in whether you get accepted over another candidate. A good way to prepare for your interview is to treat it just like the other aspects of the audition. You need to thoughtfully prepare, research, and, to a certain degree, rehearse. You cannot completely rehearse the interview, just as you cannot completely rehearse the dance portion of the audition. But you can certainly prepare for it.

Interview Prep

Knowing the program for which you are auditioning is part of your preparation for the interview. Become very familiar with not only the school but also the degree curriculum. Another important effective way to prepare for the interview is to research the school's season and see what productions they have planned. This can give you insight into the program and the school's mission. It also gives you wonderful topics of interest to discuss with your auditors. During the interview portion, relax, enjoy, and be yourself. This may be harder than it sounds, but remember that the auditors really do want to get to know you as a person.

Sample Interview Questions

- What is the department's mission?
- What is your philosophy about how to train young artists?
- Tell me about your faculty members and their special achievements
- Where are your recent graduates now, and what are they doing?
- What is the size of the freshman class, of the entire department?
- How many audition?
- What is the makeup of your student body?
- Can I double major or minor, or study abroad?
- Do freshmen get to perform on the main stage?

- What other aspects of theater can be studied?
- Do you produce student-directed productions?
- What is your season and how is it chosen?
- Who directs your shows?
- Are professional internships available?
- Do you produce a senior showcase or offer professional connections after graduation?
- Can I audit a class?
- Do you have a class on auditioning or a class on business of the business?

Questions about Other Colleges

During the interview portion of the audition, several other things can happen. Auditors may ask you what other colleges you are auditioning for. This is a practice that I frown upon but seems to be prevalent. My advice is that you do not *have* to share with the auditors the other schools that you are auditioning for. Frankly, I do not think it is any of their business or an effective use of your audition time, which in most cases is time that you have literally paid for. Often times the colleges will ask you to write down other schools that you plan to audition for. As an alternative to that, you can offer them your e-mail and agree to provide them with a complete list in writing after you have completed all your auditions. Sometimes they will ask you about other colleges when you are in the room during your audition or during the interview. I am particularly opposed to the question being asked during your interview time. I find it somewhat less objectionable when they ask you to write it down. In either case, I do not see how it is helpful to *you*. However, if that question comes up and you do not feel like you want to answer it, you certainly do not have to.

I have asked several auditors why they ask the names of other colleges students are auditioning for. Some colleges are gathering recruitment statistics. Several of the more selective colleges have told me they are simply making small talk. However, it does not seem benign to the student at the time. Students feel put on the spot as to how they should respond. If they answer honestly and list all their schools, will it hurt their chances? If they are not completely forthcoming, can they be comfortable withholding information? Which answer is the right answer?

For these awkward situations, I have a couple of suggestions. Respond by saying at that moment the only school you can think about is the school you are standing in front of and that is where you are putting your focus. Or you could just tell the auditors that you have a variety of college BA, BFA, and conservatories that you are considering without naming specific schools, and just leave it at that. The main thing to remember is that the purpose of the interview is to give the auditors an opportunity to get to know you in a more personal way beyond your monologues, songs, resume, and essay. Here is the rule of thumb: if you walk out of the audition room and feel that the auditors got to know a little something about you as a person, the interview was a success.

Chapter 5

Audition Locations

There will come a point during the application process when it is time to schedule your audition. At that point, you have several options.

On-Campus Auditions

Some schools hold auditions only on campus. The schools' Web site gives you their dates and times. Other schools have auditions on campus as well as regional off-campus auditions. Although auditioning on campus gives the college recruitment office a chance to impress you, it does not increase your chances of being admitted to the school. It does give you a firsthand look at the campus and the surrounding area. Some colleges offer complimentary tickets to see a school show if there is a performance at the time of your audition.

Off-Campus Auditions

Many schools participate in off-campus regional auditions in various cities throughout the United States. These usually begin in early fall, and some colleges continue their audition tour until late February. You will need to check the schools' Web sites to see if they are conducting auditions in a city near you. These regional auditions are often held in a hotel conference room. This can be a great convenience and money saver for your family. The National Unified Auditions are the largest regional auditions. You will find more details about Unifieds in the next chapter.

Consortium Auditions

Regional consortium auditions happen around the country. Some are on the West Coast, some are in the South, and some are in the Midwest. College representatives and auditors attend the International Thespian Convention, various state thespian conventions, the North Texas Drama Auditions, and a variety of consortium auditions around the country. These consortiums are group auditions, with twenty to fifty colleges in attendance. The college representatives are all in one room at the same time, usually a theater or convention hall. The students come in one at a time and perform their audition for all the auditors simultaneously. Most of the students have not yet applied to the colleges in attendance. Typically, the audition is ninety seconds long and strictly timed. Most students perform two monologues (for straight acting programs) or a brief monologue and forty to forty-five seconds of a song (for musical theater). When all the auditions are over, there is a callback. During the callback, no additional performance is asked of the student. The college that has called students back will encourage them to apply to their school. The auditors might want to see the students in a more extended audition setting, such as their campus or one of their regional auditions, to perform additional songs or monologues. They may need to see students dance or have additional faculty members meet them. In some cases the auditors will actually offer an artistic acceptance on the spot for acting, musical theater, or vocal performance programs during the call back. This really depends on the recruitment style of the individual college.

Prescreen Audition

Because of the increased number of applicants, some of the more popular schools have begun prescreening candidates. It is a very smart way, I think, for colleges to narrow down the list of auditionees to those most likely to be a good fit for their university. In these cases, the colleges request an electronic or live prescreen submission prior to granting an in-person audition. The University of Oklahoma Department of Musical Theater conducts artistic prescreens in person, as well as via DVD submissions. Otterbein University and NYU/Steinhardt also require an artistic electronic prescreen. Texas State University has implemented an artistic electronic prescreen. The University of Michigan and Indiana University conduct both an academic and artistic prescreen for musical theatre. Artistic prescreens usually take the form of a mailed-in DVD of performance requirements, or an electronic submission via email or an upload to an online service. Your submission can be something simple that you record at home, or you could hire a professional videographer. Complete guidelines are available on the college websites.

DVD/Digital Audition

If you are unable to get to the campus for an audition, a growing number of colleges allow you to do your complete college audition via a DVD submission. This is not the same as the prescreen. It simply takes the place of an in-person audition. I expect a trend toward more colleges accepting DVD and digital audition submissions as the applicant pool continues to increase. As of this writing, New York University's Tisch School of the Arts accepts a digital audition submitted as an e-mail attachment and a live interview over the Internet via Skype. This may seem an unusual venue for an audition, but I have been interacting with students all over the country via Skype and iChat for years with great success. I have also preliminarily introduced some of my students to college auditors using their Youtube performances. The Internet provides a form of communication that we are becoming accustomed to. When an in-person audition and interview are not possible, an electronic submission provides a viable alternative.

Chapter 6

The National Unified Auditions

Three different college theater educators from three different universities got together some years back and cofounded the National Unified Auditions to accommodate large numbers of students who are auditioning for multiple colleges. Those pioneer gentlemen were, and still are, Charley Helfert from Southern Methodist University, Peter Sargeant from Webster University, and John David Lutz from the University of Evansville.

Universities that are National Unified member schools and offer undergraduate degrees in acting and musical theater programs convene in the same city on the same dates and hold their auditions. Each individual college holds its auditions separately in a hotel meeting room or at nearby locations or studios. Unlike the consortium concept, where all the auditors from all the colleges are in the same room, the National Unified Auditions are held separately and privately by each member school. These auditions begin in late January and continue until mid-February.

At the time of this writing, there were twenty-five National Unified member colleges, universities, and conservatories. Auditors from these schools travel to New York for two days, Chicago for three days, Los Angeles for two days, and Las Vegas for two days. There has been some discussion about adding additional cities and dates. When you apply for admission and schedule your audition for a Unified member school, you may choose an off-campus Unified Audition site for convenience. Simply pick the city (New York, Chicago, Los Angeles, or Las Vegas) in which you want to schedule your audition. The individual colleges have these locations and dates listed on their Web sites.

Auditioning through the Unified system has many benefits: it saves you money and time auditioning a number of times while having to travel to only one city. I prefer the Chicago and Los Angeles sites for several reasons. Most of the colleges hold their auditions at the same hotel. Only a couple of colleges conduct their auditions at a nearby hotel or dance studio. For the majority of the auditions, you do not need to catch a cab or drive anywhere; you simply go down the elevator to the appropriate meeting room, assuming that you are staying in the hotel. It is very easy and stress free. Chicago is the only site where the Unified schools hold auditions for three days. The other cities have only two days of auditions. In Chicago you have that third day to get more auditions in.

Parents sometimes express concern about their child getting sick during the audition season and fear that having several auditions on the same date is too risky. I have a wonderful anecdote regarding illness during auditions. One of my students had a scheduled audition for the University of Michigan at Chicago Unifieds and she was ill. We pushed her audition to late in the afternoon, giving her as much time to recover as possible and made the auditors aware of her condition. She handled it like a pro, performed the best she could and made no excuses. They were extremely impressed with her talent AND her attitude, and subsequently accepted her into their BFA musical theatre program. Her auditor that day was University of Michigan professor, Mark Madama. Mark tells this story in his podcast interview which can be found on my website at www.collegeauditioncoach.com. He thought that if she performed so well while being sick, imagine how well she could perform at 100%! It made quite an impression.

Every year I attend the Unified Auditions in Chicago and Los Angeles with my students and have been doing do since 2005. I feel it is a very effective method for auditioning for multiple schools.

National Unified Audition Member Schools

University of the Arts

Ball State University

Boston Conservatory

University of Cincinnati

Cornish College of the Arts

Emerson College

University of Evansville

The Hartt School, University of Hartford

Ithaca College

University of Miami

University of Michigan

Montclair State University

Northern Illinois University

University of Oklahoma

Otterbein College

Pennsylvania State University

Point Park University

Roosevelt University

College of Santa Fe

Southern Methodist University

Texas Christian University

University of Utah

Viterbo University

Webster University

Something very interesting happens during the Unified Auditions. A large number of nonmember colleges also hold their regional off-campus auditions in the same cities as the Unifieds on the same days. So the total number of colleges that are actually available for you to audition for is more like fifty. In attendance are the twenty-five Unified schools I have listed and another twenty or so schools that piggyback on the Unified dates. You have the opportunity to audition for many more schools. Those additional colleges are usually in the same hotel as well, or in the immediate neighborhood. Just like as Unified member colleges do, these colleges require that you apply first. Then you can schedule your audition in the city and date that is going to coincide with the Unified day. Scheduling the audition is all part of the application process. There is no central Unified audition scheduler. These appointments are made through the individual colleges as you apply.

Just another note: When you do get to Unifieds, many of the additional nonmember schools will accept walk-ins. You can simply go to the room where the college is holding its auditions and ask if it is taking any walk-ins. You do not have to have apply to the college ahead of time. If the auditors have room to see you, they will let you audition. The important thing to remember is that there is no guarantee that you will be able to secure a walk-in audition. It is on a first come, first served basis. Most of the walk-in schools require an audition fee. The fees vary from school to school but range from $25 to $100, so bring your checkbook.

Unifieds Packing List

This is the list I give my students and parents before Unified auditions:

- If you have not already done so, *reread the plays* your monologues are from.

- Update your resume.

- Clean up your Facebook profile, and never post college acceptances or scholarships awards on your public profile.

- Pack backup audition outfit.

- MTers might want to pack a personal steamer.

- Pack a travel-size hand sanitizer.

- Bring about twenty head shots and resumes (stapled).

- Pack your performance journal.

- Pack thank-you cards and stamps.

- MTers: bring a small portable CD player or iPod with dock, and pack extra batteries. Schools do not provide a player for your recorded tracks!. For those with live accompaniment, be sure your sheet music is correctly prepped. Make sure your dance attire is appropriate.

- Pack water bottle and take it with you to all auditions. Sip throughout the day (and on airplane) to relieve muscle tension in voice box. Do not yell or talk too loudly.

- Pack note cards on why you want to attend each college so you can discuss it during the interview.

- Facebook friend former students and ask any college questions.

- Get plenty of rest, and watch your diet/nutrition/exercise. Do not do anything stupid like drink alcohol. You need to be at the top of your game.

- The Palmer House Hilton has an excellent gym. Bring appropriate attire if you want to work out.

- Post Unified photos, discussions, acceptances, and info only on our private Facebook group, not on your public profile.

- Time your pieces again to be sure they are in accordance with the guidelines of each college.

- Listen to all the podcast interviews on my Web site to prep for interview.

- Pack your positive mental program!

Chapter 7

Choosing Monologue Material

Type Matters

The most important thing to consider when choosing monologue material for your college audition is your castable type. The colleges are most likely going to be casting a company of actors, and it is unlikely that they will accept many students of the same type. Even if they are not casting a company, they will perceive you as a type as soon as you enter the room. You need to play to your strengths by choosing material that supports your individual type.

Say you are short, stout, and freckled face and have a big smile, great big eyes, and curly red hair. The auditors are going to perceive you as a character actor, so you need to have material that supports that castable type. For girls in musical theater, if you are a character type, you especially need to be show your belt because those character girl musical roles are written in large part for a belt or a mix/blend. In plays, character roles tend to be comic roles or outside the mainstream in some way, so your monologue material should reflect that. If you are a tall, thin, beautiful, fair-skinned female MTer, you are going to be expected to sing with a beautiful legit soprano and play leading-lady roles. These are important things to consider when choosing material.

Monologue Guidelines

Most of the colleges want two contrasting monologues. Some schools require that one of the monologues be classical, but the majority of schools, for musical theater especially, are going to want two contemporary, contrasting monologues. Contrasting does not necessarily mean comic and dramatic. As long as the selections have a distinctly different tone, you will have met that requirement. For straight acting programs, the majority of the colleges are going to request one classical and one contemporary monologue. Many musical theater programs require only one monologue. If that is the case, find a piece with an emotional arch to show two tones.

Classical Monologues

A classical monologue is from a play that was written before 1900, beginning with the Greeks. Some material from popular playwrights of that general period—such as Oscar Wilde, George Bernard Shaw, Henrik Ibsen, and Anton Chekhov—might be a good choice for an additional or third monologue. For your initial classical monologue, I recommend that you stay away from those particular playwrights because their writings in large part were done around the turn of the twentieth century, so they sit right on the edge of the time line. I have success sticking with traditional classical playwrights such as Shakespeare, Calderon, Sophocles (in verse), and Moliere.

It is important that you carefully and specifically market yourself to the colleges. Even though you are an actor who has range and can perform a lot more than just one style and one type of acting, do not try to show *all* these qualities to the colleges. You need to showcase who you primarily are, your essence. Once you get accepted into the college, then you can spread your wings and begin to show your range over the four years. The initial audition is not the time to show your range. You need to stay within your castable type. Read the quotes from college auditors at the end of this book and you will see that they want to see who you are right now and how they can cast you. Although it is important to show some contrast *within* your castable type, you should not go *outside* the range of your castable type. The best rule of thumb when choosing material: the material should be something you could be cast in right now, today. The only time you will be playing roles far outside your age range is in high school. For college auditions you need to think on a national scale because the auditors are evaluating you in that context. You will be cast as Ophelia, not Lady Macbeth.

Classical Playwrights

I mentioned earlier my success with using Moliere and Shakespeare. I particularly like Moliere because of the excellent contemporary translations from the French by Richard Wilbur. Obviously with Shakespeare, you have a limited number of choices. Shakespeare wrote only so many plays with only so many roles for women and only so many roles for men. And with Shakespeare you will not be dealing with the translation, so the language hurdle is a bit higher although not insurmountable. I find that most high school seniors are not familiar with performing classical material, and it can present certain problems. That is just something to consider when choosing classical material. You are probably going to have to spend more time working on it and preparing it. The colleges that require classical material have their own reasons for requesting it. Carnegie Mellon specifically states in its audition requirements that auditors would like classical material with a special concentration on language. These colleges want to see how you handle the verse. You can certainly fulfill that requirement with Shakespeare. Be sure the Shakespeare you choose is written in iambic pentameter and not in prose. Moliere is a good choice because he wrote in iambic pentameter and rhyming couplets, so the verse requirement will be fulfilled. Remember that not all classical material is written in verse, and not all translations are in verse form. If you decide on the works of some of the popular Greek playwrights (Socrates, Euripides, or Aristophanes), be sure the translation you choose is in verse.

Contemporary Monologues

A contemporary monologue is from a play written from 1900 to the present day. That leaves a very large span of time from which to choose material. For my own students, I prefer monologues from plays written within the last five to ten years. I think it is important for young students to recognize playwrights from their own generation. If you choose a play from the 1960s, '70s, or '80s, there is a chance it is going to be either overdone or something the auditors feel is a bit stale. When I think contemporary, I think fresh and modern.

Classic, Not ClassiCAL Material

Classic material written by the great modern writers of the twentieth century would include Arthur Miller, Eugene O'Neill, William Inge, and William Saroyan. Those playwrights are a wonderful source for contemporary monologues as long as you pick something that is from one of their lesser-known works and not something that is done too often. There is really nothing wrong with doing material that the auditors have heard before. It is just always nice when someone walks in with material that the auditors have not thought of for a long time. "Oh I love that play. I haven't thought of that play in a long time." Or "I'm not familiar with that particular one-act by that playwright." I once gave a monologue from an obscure William Inge play to a student for her Carnegie Mellon audition. It became an engaging conversation starter during the interview because the auditor was not familiar with the play but loved the playwright. By now you should understand the definitions of classical and contemporary and the differences between the two and the importance of finding the right material to showcase you.

Finding Monologues

Now I want to address how you are going to go about finding your actual monologues. I can give you some suggestions of what I do and how I feel about seeking the right material for my students. It is time for you to become aware of plays and playwrights. The smart way to do that is to begin reading plays and going to the theater. Sometimes my students tell me they do not know where to begin. Learning how to find material is something that you need to become somewhat of an expert at because you are always going to be auditioning. Part of growing into a mature artist is learning how to do this on your own. When you are a senior in high school, you may not be familiar with how to search for appropriate college audition material. I spend a large part of my time doing just that. But I also train my students how to find material so that once they leave me and go on to college, they have some tools to use to find appropriate audition repertoire.

Begin by going to the theater and by reading plays. Go to your public library's play section, and read anything that looks interesting with characters that are your age and type. Another good beginning source is to investigate different colleges and look at their seasons to see what plays they are performing. You will begin to familiarize yourself with various playwrights. Also, go to the regional theaters' Web sites around the country and look at their seasons; see what plays they are producing. It is important to regularly read playbill.com and nytimes.com theater section and see what shows are being done on Broadway and off Broadway. Another helpful source for young, up-and-coming playwrights is New Dramatists. At newdramatists.org, you can find wonderful young writers of all ethnicities who are writing about their experiences and their cultures. It is a wonderful way to find material, especially if you are Asian, African American, or Hispanic. I think you will find some writers that really speak to you. You should be marketing yourself, as I said earlier, for the kind of type you will be playing and how you will be cast. If you are an ethnic minority, it is very important that you find pieces that suit you and promote that wonderful, unique quality that you bring. The ND playwrights are excellent for that.

Another wonderful way to find monologues is to go to Karen Kohlhaas's Web site, www.monologueaudition.com. Karen, a professor at the Atlantic Acting School at New York University, has a very helpful list of suggested monologues and another list of overdone monologues. I think it is a great idea to scan through that list. Additionally, Karen has a book, *How to Choose a Monologue for Any Audition,* which is a must-have for all actors. This book is a complete and thorough guide on how to find appropriate monologue material for any number of audition occasions.

If you happen to be in New York City, visit the Drama Bookshop in Midtown. I can spend a whole afternoon there. The bookstore has a section called New Plays, and you can just sit there cross-legged on the floor and read through all the new plays there, finding appropriate material that fits you. There is always a helpful sales associate to answer questions and make suggestions.

The way to begin with a new play, classical or contemporary, is to look at the cast of characters to see if there is an age-appropriate character in the play that you could portray (a character from fourteen to fifteen years old all the way up to mid to late twenties, depending on how old you look). Once you determine if there is actually a character for you, then go through the play to see if the character has a monologue. You do not always have to find a monologue that is already written in monologue form. Many times you can piece together lines from a scene to form a monologue.

A strong need on the part of the character makes a good monologue. Avoid narrative monologues or storytelling, "once upon a time this happened to me" monologues. These usually lack a strong need or can be too emotionally passive and reflective. The character you are portraying must really need something from the person the character is talking to. Do not choose anything that is overly dramatic or overly emotional. Simple is better. Material that serves you best is thoughtful and compelling that fits your type. The most common mistake that high school students make is overtrying and showing too much in the audition. The auditors have conducted hundreds, and in some cases thousands, of auditions, and they are a bit weary and emotionally drained. Auditors are more likely to be captivated by an actor who is honestly connected to material that is well suited to him or her and uncomplicated. You have a short period to perform for the auditors, and it is not possible in that short time to show them everything you can do. It is better that you show one thing you can do well. In the case of your college audition, less is more.

Know Your Castable Type

I have fifteen years of experience as a casting director, so I am very familiar with being on the other side of the table. You are going to be sized up right away by type. Auditors are going to take one look at you and start assessing how they can cast you. So it is important for you to know your castable type. You need to talk about your type with people who know you, your directors, acting teachers, and other actors. You should begin to learn how others see you and embrace the type that you are. If you are a tall, handsome, well-built actor, chances are you are going to be seen as a leading man. If you are short and stocky, with curly hair red hair and freckles, you will be seen as a character actor. Prepare your material accordingly. You need to affirm in the auditors' minds by your choice of material exactly who they see come in the door. If they see consistency in material and type, then things make sense and there is no confusion as to how to cast you.

Having said that, you do need to show range. You can show plenty of range and still stay within your castable type. For example, your first monologue might be combative and confrontational, and your second monologue might have a tone that is vulnerable and tender. Both monologues will be contrasting but within your castable type. You do not want to do Blanche from *A Streetcar Named Desire* or Willy Loman from *Death of a Salesman* if you are a high school senior. Those characters are not appropriate for your age and experience.

If you are auditioning for musical theater, it is important that your songs be well coordinated with your monologues. All of your material needs to send the same consistent message to the auditors of what type you are. And if you are a character type, they expect to hear you belt. Yes, you need to show some vocal variety, but you do not want to go outside your castable type. This applies to your head shots as well. The way you are dressed, your songs, your monologues, everything needs to send the same message to the auditors about who you are and how you can be cast. Colleges are thinking ahead about how to market you to agents, casting directors, and managers upon your graduation.

Profanity

The question of using profanity in monologues is something that comes up occasionally when I am coaching, mainly with parents. Here is my feeling about it. The auditors will not be offended by profanity if it is not excessive or gratuitous. However, it is important that *you* be comfortable with any expletives in your monologue. If my actor is uncomfortable with profanity, I make adjustments. I never give a student a monologue that is so offensive it would actually hurt his or her chances of getting admitted to a college. Some colleges are more conservative in their taste than others are, and that is something that I take into consideration. You might want to use the same monologue and clean it up a little bit for a conservative school and then perform it uncensored for other schools.

It is important to note that there are auditors who take more offense at changing or censoring a playwright's words than actually hearing the profanity itself. If the profanity has a place in the language of the monologue and if it is important for the character and what the character needs, then we keep it in the monologue. By in large, college auditors are not offended by profanity that is a necessary part of the text. But it is probably not a good idea to angrily scream the "F-bomb" over and over again. In such a case, the mistake of being too emotionally charged is the culprit rather than the profanity itself.

Chapter 8

Preparing Your Monologue

When I begin with a student on monologue preparation, I break the work down into three sections: text analysis, application of the text analysis, and performing the monologue.

Text Analysis

When you woke up today, you did not just fall out of bed and float aimlessly through the day. You had things you wanted to accomplish, things that motivated you to put one foot in front of the other. The characters in the plays are no different. It is your sole responsibility, as an actor, to get inside the head of the character and figure out what motivated the character to get out of bed. Why did he or she put one foot in front of the other?

You must know the answers to three important questions before you start on any acting work: Who am I? What do I want? What do I do to get what I want? The first question applies to the character. The second, to the character's objective. The third, to the character's action. These basic fundamentals of acting technique are taught today the same way they were taught when I went to acting school at the American Conservatory Theater back in the mid-1970s.

I was recently invited to sit in on some acting classes at Carnegie Mellon. Professor Barbara Mackenzie-Wood and I discussed with the class the fact that no one has reinvented the wheel, so to speak. The technique that was taught years ago is still the same solid technique that is taught today at Carnegie Mellon and in classrooms around the country. The nomenclature might be different, but the general technique remains the same. You may hear an "objective" called "intention" or "goal." You may hear "actions" called "tactics" or "beats." But the idea remains the same.

A character will also have a "super objective," which is what he or she wants over the whole life of the play, regardless of circumstance. Good examples of this are something sweeping in scope such as *I want justice* or *I want control* or *I want to avoid responsibility*. The super objective is the first thing that you need to understand about the character you are playing. A good guide to finding a character's super objective is to keep asking the question why when considering the character's behavior. The next thing to consider is the objective in the scene in which the monologue is from. Sometimes I refer to that as the "mini objective." Next, you need to plot the actions that feed into that mini objective. The actions play into the mini objective and the mini objective feeds into the super objective.

Objectives

What do I want?
To better illustrate how to break down text, I find it helpful to use made-up scenarios based on my experiences and those of my students. These serve as examples that illustrate how to use objectives and actions. I begin with an example from my life.

Let us say that I am going to the grocery store. It is *never* just a trip to the grocery store. Let us look deeper. Let us say I am going to Whole Foods to purchase items for a recipe that I have carefully chosen as a part of a menu that I am preparing. Let us say I am shopping for farm-raised salmon, organic fruits, vine-ripe vegetables, and fresh herbs. I then prepare the meal and gather my family together to share each other's company at the dining room table so that I can prove my worth as a wife and a mother. So it is never just a trip to the grocery store. There is always something else going on underneath the actions. How aware am I of proving my worth as a wife and a mother when I go to Whole Foods? I am probably not thinking about that at all. Yet it is very much living inside me all the time whether I am aware of it or not.

Similarly, I tell my students that when they got up in the morning, there was something living inside of them motivating them. After my grocery store example, I build a scenario using my students. Let us call the scenario, The Life and Times of (fill in the blank).

For this example, we will use the name John Doe. Let us say John's super objective is that he wants independence. Let us also say that John has a curfew of midnight on the weekends. This particular weekend John is invited to a party with some older friends who go to the college and do not have a curfew because they live in apartments or dormitories where they do not have to answer to a parent. John wants to stay out over the weekend and go to this party and not have to go home at midnight. He knows that his mother will be apprehensive about letting him stay out all night.

John goes into the kitchen to talk to his mother. His objective is *to get his curfew extended.* He is armed with whatever tactics he thinks will help him get his way. The scene goes like this: He says, "Why, mother you look so gorgeous today, you are simply glowing. I love what you are wearing. It makes you look so thin. By the way, how about lifting my curfew for the weekend?"

When John walked into the kitchen, what his objective? His objective was *to get his curfew lifted.* And what was his first action? His first action was *to flatter.* Mother's response is to thank John for being so sweet and complimentary, but she says no to having his curfew lifted, that she expects him home at midnight.

John tried his first action but did not get what he wanted. Will he give up? No! He will not give up because he really wants to go to the party and because his super objective is that he wants independence. And in the most basic terms, his want is greater than the obstacle that has been put in front of him. So if he does not get what he wants and does not give up, what will he do? He will try a second action.

Now John says to his mother, "I'll tell you what I'll do. I'll take out the garbage, bathe the dogs, do the dishes, and mow the lawn for the rest of the month if you'll let me stay out late for this party, just this one time." Mother's response is that she could really use more help around the house, but she will not give John any extra privilege for it.

The second action is *to negotiate*. However, it did not get John what he wants. Will he give up? No! So now John tries a third action. Now he is more frustrated and says, "Oh, well, that's just great Mother, that's really great. I'll be the only one who has to come home at midnight when everybody else gets to stay out as late as they want to. You'll humiliate and embarrass me in front of all my friends." Let us call that third action *to shame*. Mother's retort is to tell John that his other friends are not her concern. The rules are the rules, and she is not letting him stay out all night regardless of what everybody else is doing.

Wow! Okay, so now John Doe has tried three actions: *flattery, negotiating,* and *shaming*. None is working. It is getting harder for John to achieve his objective. So now John might have to do something called *raising the stakes*. This means heightening his need so that he tries harder to get what he wants. One way to think of it is to try to imagine what would happen if John does not get what he wants. The scene would end. The curtain would come down. They play would be over. The audience would go home and wonder why they paid $175 a ticket to see *The Life and Times of John Doe*. They could have just stayed home and watched *American Idol!*

Here is something important that I learned early in my training and have never forgotten. One of my acting teachers at the American Conservatory Theater was Paul Blake (now executive director of the MUNY in Saint Louis). He told me that playwrights write plays only about people who *really* want things. Playwrights do not write plays and musicals about people who kind of want something. Plays involve great big wants and needs. Otherwise, we would all stay home and watch television. You have to assume when you are playing a role that the character's objectives are enormously important to the character. This is true of every play, every script, and every musical.

So let us go back to the John Doe scene. The first three actions have been shot down. Things are getting harder, so now John will raise the stakes for himself because he must keep fighting. This is a play and the character had great big wants. Say that a certain girl will be at this party. This girl is someone that John is very interested in seeing. She is a sophomore in college, and if he does not see her this weekend, he will not see her until spring break. He has been Facebook chatting, Skyping, and texting her. He has even bought a new pair of blue jeans for the party. Nothing will keep him from going to this party, seeing this girl, and staying out as late as he wants. Aha! Now he has a reason to keep fighting. Now he has raised the stakes.

At this point John tries a fourth action, *to beg*. He falls to his knees, clasps his hands together, and pleads, "Please, I am begging you. I'll do anything you ask, but for God's sake just this one time. Please, please, please. You've got to let me stay out all weekend!" His mother says, "All right, John, get up off your knees. You've worn me down. Okay, okay you can go. But I want you to call me at midnight and tell me where you're spending the night." John jumps up and down with joy, hugs his mother, and says, "You're the best mother ever!" He got what he wanted. Objective achieved!

The reason for the aforementioned example is this: When you walk into the room for your college audition, your auditor will expect interesting and specific choices that add levels, depth, texture, and richness to your performance. The actions give your performance layers, levels, and depth.

What if you had played that entire scene using the one action of begging? It would have been boring and one dimensional. Back at your high school, when your world was palm sized, a successful performance was defined by knowing your lines and blocking; getting your laugh line; hitting that money note; getting a standing ovation and praises from parents, students, and teachers. It is now time for you to be critiqued on a national scale. The college auditors will scrutinize you more carefully than you have ever been scrutinized before. This requires that you raise the level of your performance. Without a solid acting technique that includes clearly planned objectives and actions, it is unlikely that you can compete successfully for college admissions at these elite BA and BFA programs. The auditors expect to see thoughtfully prepared material that you are fully connected to.

Another helpful technique to add to the actions is the use of an adverb. An example would be if you *timidly* beg or *obnoxiously* beg. Adding the adverb ties in the character and makes your acting choice more specific.

Let us go back to the life and times of John Doe. John is a nice guy, but let us say he has an evil twin brother. If evil John and nice John are given the same objective and the same actions, would they play the scene differently? The answer is yes because there are two different characters. This is where the use of an adverb can be helpful.

By adding an adverb to the action, you can accomplish three things: connect the character to the action, make what you are playing more specific, and give yourself an emotional anchor. The evil Jon character might beg obnoxiously, whereas the nice John character might beg earnestly. So adding the adverb not only gives you something extra to play but also makes your performance more specific and ties in the character. Sometimes using an adverb can help if you are playing a particularly long action. If the action spans a large part of dialogue in the monologue, you might want to simply assign two different adverbs to the action. These adverbs can empower your character toward achieve his or her objective.

Actions

What do I do to get what I want? How do you break down the monologue into actions? Visualize the John Doe scene as a digital file. We have three actions: *flattering, negotiating,* and *begging.* We will pull your college audition monologue out of that scene. Now it has to stand alone as a monologue. It has to make sense by itself outside of the scene. It has to have a through line that tells a complete story outside the context of the play. The monologue might encompass only one of the actions within the scene, right? But you cannot play it that way because it will be flat, uninteresting, and one dimensional. What we will do is inject all three of those actions into the monologue. The monologue becomes a condensed version of the scene. It becomes its own little miniplay, which is really what it has to be to stand alone for your audition. The length of most monologues for college auditions is between one and two minutes. For a typical one-to-two-minute monologue, playing three or four actions is the ideal number for your character to achieve his or her objective. Five actions are too many, and two are not enough to show variety and levels. So break down your monologue into three or four actions. This next section on application of the text analysis explains how.

Application of the Text Analysis

Here is how to apply the text analysis to the actual acting of the monologue. First, get your monologue photocopied on a piece of paper because you will be making notes that you will need to refer to as you learn the monologue. At the top of the monologue, write your character's super objective. Then write down what your character wants in the scene (mini objective).

If we use *The Life and Times of John Doe*, the super objective written at the top of the page would be *wants independence*. The mini objective is *to get curfew lifted*. Write the actions of the monologue in the margins. On the first three or four sentences, John flatters, so write *to flatter* outside the margins of those lines. Then bracket the next section of the lines. On these lines he negotiates, so write *to negotiate* in the margin. Then the next group of lines assign to the section on *begging* and so forth. You now have all of the actions clearly marked so you know exactly on which line the action starts and exactly on which line it ends. Then add the adverbs as you continue.

That is the basic structure for how to apply the text analysis to the text itself. It is very important that you write it on the actual piece of paper that your monologue is photocopied on so that you have it to refer to when you are rehearsing and learning your lines. This is very similar to how you would diagram a sentence.

To begin the actual application of the text analysis, I have my students sit across from me and look me right in the eye and take the monologue action by action. They give me the lines of the first action while playing the action. If the first action is *to exuberantly compliment*, the student looks at me in the eyes and says those lines exuberantly complimenting me. Then we stop. Then the student states the next action, for example, *to shamelessly negotiate*. Then the student says the lines that are assigned to that action right to me. We continue this throughout the monologue. If I feel that my student is not connecting with the action, I will have her or him do it over and over and over again until we feel as though the student is really connected with playing the chosen action. Then we set the actions for performance. Once we are satisfied with connection to the actions, I get my students up on their feet and we begin the actual staging of the monologue.

It is all right to change your action (or your objective or super objective) if you feel as though it is not working for you. But once you have decided on an action, stay with it and commit to it completely before abandoning it to try another action. Do not discard it unless you feel as though it is absolutely not helping you get what you want.

You need to focus on the person you are talking to, clearly see that person, and then perform the actions to that person all the while trying to get what you want from that person. In that exercise we do not state what the actions are right before we do them. The student simply performs the actions without stating them. If at any time I feel as though again the actor is not connecting with the actions, we go back to step one, which is stating the action and then saying the words that are a part of that action.

Once you have successfully stood up, found a place on the other side of the room to focus on the person you are talking to, and have performed the actions fully connected, the next step is to bridge the actions with transitions. The transitions tie the actions together. Why do we change our actions? We change our actions because of what we are or are not getting from the other person. So we have a string of actions, but we cannot just blindly jump from one action to the other action without any connection. This is where the transitions come in.

The only way to get to the next action is to focus on the other person, the person whom you are talking to. You need to see that person. What is his or her reaction? Turning away to walk out of the room? Laughing at you? Spitting in you face? Smirking? Leaning forward to really take an interest in what you are saying? That reaction from the person you are talking to is what is propels you into the next action. You cannot manufacture that on your own as an actor. You have got to depend on what you are getting from the other person and let that propel you. The other person's reaction is where your transition comes from.

Doing monologues is tricky because you do not have the other person there. You stand alone talking to a spot on the back wall and trying to connect to it. It is up to you to use your imagination to really see the person whom you are talking to in this scene. Really imagine what that person's reaction is and how it feeds you into your next action. That is how you build the little bridges of transition from one action to the next. It can take a while to perfect this. It is a long process of repetition. I rehearse this with my students countless times. When you are rehearsing your piece, you need to do this over and over again.

Once you have a thoughtful super objective, mini objective, clear and succinct actions you are connected to, helpful adverbs, and all your transitions, and you clearly see whom you are talking to, you are ready to perform. Now you can begin memorizing your lines.

Performing the Monologue

Realize that you will be in an audition room. It could be a dance studio, it could be a theater, it could be a classroom, it could be a hotel room, or it could be a hotel ballroom. You have to be able to adjust to the room where you will perform. There are two important things to remember. First, find a spot on the back wall above the heads of your auditors that you can focus on clearly and easily. That will be the person you are talking to. Do not look your auditors directly in the eye during your monologue. The other thing is to imagine a line in front of you that you do not cross so that you do not get into the space of the auditors. Find a comfortable amount of space to perform your monologue in without going all over the room and without getting too close into the space of the auditors. Imagine that space for yourself when you stage your monologue, and be sure that you are able to focus above the heads of the auditors on a wall opposite you. And remember that you have to be heard. If you perform in a theater, you need to project far enough that the auditors can hear you. If you have a quiet, intimate moment in the monologue, you also need to be aware that if you get too quiet, the auditors will not to be able to hear you. Adjust your volume accordingly to the size of the room.

Introduce your monologues in the following manner. For a contemporary monologue, state the name of the play and the playwright. Do not state the character you are portraying. For a classical monologue, state the name of the play and the character you are portraying. Do not state the playwright. If you are doing Benedick from *Much Ado About Nothing*, assume your auditors know that William Shakespeare wrote *Much Ado*.

You do not need to introduce yourself unless it is a very formal audition. If the auditors already have your picture and resume and you have walked into the room and shaken their hands and they have said, "Hi, John," you do not need to introduce the audition with, "Hello, my name is John Doe. For my first monologue I will be performing blah, blah, blah." They already know who you are. Use your noggin. Be present in the room. If the room has a relaxed vibe, you can relax a little. If the room is very formal, you might want to introduce yourself a little more formally, maybe shake hands. You need to use your head when you enter the room.

Your audition starts the moment you open the door. You need to let the auditors know how glad you are to be there. Be bright, happy, and positive. Sometimes actors look as though they are afraid, and that gives the wrong impression. Remember that this is what you love to do! This is your passion. You are so thrilled to be there to share your artistry and perform these wonderful monologues. Smile, hand the auditors your head shot and resume, shake their hands if you feel it is appropriate, and announce your pieces in the order that you are going to perform them. Then give the auditors a second to settle because they may be writing down the names of your pieces. After the auditors settle, take about four seconds to review your objectives and actions. Then look up, find the place to focus on the person you are talking to, breath, and begin the monologue.

When you finish the monologue, *do not say thank you.* It seems cursory and insincere and makes you look nervous. The auditors know that you are grateful. At the end of your monologue, hold for three or four seconds and then break. Look at your auditors and smile. They will know that you are finished. When your entire audition is over and you are exiting the room, then thank the auditors for their time. Tell them how wonderful it was to meet them, what an enjoyable experience you had, and that you hope they have a wonderful rest of their day. Then pat yourself on your back for a job well done.

Chapter 9

Mock Auditions

Get Audition Ready

Once your audition material has been chosen, prepared, and rehearsed, you need to get "audition ready." This means being fully prepared and ready with your songs and monologues, interview skills, head shot, resume, and wardrobe.

Over the years I have learned that the best way to prepare my students for their actual performance is through a series of mock auditions. I conduct these mock auditions throughout the year in various cities around the country with experienced auditors. It is important that you feel confident in your material and that you feel relaxed, comfortable, and ready to perform when the real audition day comes. Auditioning, like it or not, is still the process by which colleges decide which students will be the best fit for their selective theater programs. Finding a way to be at ease in that situation is something that can best be achieved through dress rehearsing it in a mock setting. You can ask your high school drama teacher or choir teacher to allow you to rehearse your pieces in a mock setting in a classroom. If that is not an option for you, perform your audition for your family and friends whenever possible.

When you participate in a mock audition, rehearse completely and thoroughly. This includes walking into the room, wearing your audition outfit with head shot and resume in hand. The mock audition, as with a real audition, starts from the moment the door opens. Include how you approach the auditors' table, how you introduce yourself, and how you end the audition and exit the room. If you will be singing, consider how you relate to the accompanist and set the tempo. (I included details on working with the accompanist in chapter 3.) If you will be using recorded tracks, be sure your player is cued and the volume is set and that you have fresh batteries. If you will be using an iPod, be sure your playlist is cued and ready and volume set. Additionally, it is very important that you rehearse your mock in the outfit you will be wearing, including shoes, hair, and—for girls—makeup. How you present yourself, your personality, when you walk into the room, and how you greet your auditors and announce your pieces is just as important to rehearse as your monologue and songs are.

During my mocks, students watch each other perform, and the auditors give oral critiques after the audition. Hearing different critiques is also a good reminder that there will be as many different opinions of your audition as there are colleges and further emphasizes how subjective the audition process is. It is a good idea to start participating in mock auditions as soon as you have your performance material ready. Participate in as many mocks as possible. It will build your confidence better than anything I know.

Chapter 10

Resumes, Head Shots, and Wardrobe

Your Resume

Your resume is primarily a representation of your performance credits and may include experience in related fields. You should present your performance resume to the auditors at all your auditions. A performance resume should be only one page.

The top of the page needs to have a heading with your name, height, weight, eye color hair color, e-mail address, and cell phone contact information. Also with the heading, I like an insert of your head shot, postage-stamp size. This allows the auditors to see who you are without having to constantly flip over your resume to look at the head shot. I also prefer the three-column format for your performance credits. The far left column indicates the name of the production; the center column, the name of the role you played; the right hand column presents the venue where you performed the show. Credits need to be listed in descending order from most recent (beginning at freshman year, no earlier). Training needs to be under a separate heading: voice lessons, acting lessons, dance lessons. An optional special abilities heading (speaking a foreign language, playing a musical instrument) or special honors could be at the very bottom of your resume.

Black-and-white resumes are a bit old-fashioned now that we have switched to color head shots. Putting some color on your resume is a good idea as long as it is not distracting. I suggest you print your name and your headings in a color that complements your postage-stamp-sized head shot insert.

Be sure your resume is well organized and easy to read. A standard sheet of paper is slightly larger than an eight-by-ten head shot, so you will need to trim the resume to fit your picture. And staple it (facing out) to the back of your head shot. Here is an example of what I consider a well-prepared college audition resume. You can't see color here, but the headings are a dark teal color that matches her blouse.

PAM COVINGTON

E-mail address
Height:	4'11"	Hair:	Blonde
Weight:	92 lbs	Eyes:	Brown

THEATRICAL EXPERIENCE
(Professional and Student Productions)

The Crucible	Mary Warren	The Hockaday School
La Casa de Bernarda Alba	Bernarda Alba*	The Hockaday School
The Real Inspector Hound	Moon*	The Hockaday School
And Then They Came for Me	Eva Geringer*	Dallas Children's Theater
Metamorphoses	Various	The Hockaday School
The Giver	Fiona	Dallas Children's Theater
Street Scene	Alice Simpson	The Hockaday School
The Sound of Music	Gretl	The Hockaday School
After Juliet	Bianca	The Hockaday School
The Miracle Worker	Helen Keller*	Dallas Children's Theater
The Secret Garden	Mary Lennox*	Dallas Children's Theater
The Music Man	Winthrop	The Hockaday School
To Kill a Mockingbird	Scout*	Dallas Children's Theater
Sarah, Plain and Tall	Rose	Dallas Children's Theater
The Island of the Skog	Skog	Dallas Children's Theater

TRAINING

British American Drama Academy	
Midsummer Conservatory - Oxford	2009 Summer
	Acting - Classical; Shakespeare
Mary Anna Dennard	2006-present
	Monologue Coach
The Hockaday School	2006-present
	Acting; Improv; Dance
Dallas Children's Theater	1996-present
	Acting

AWARDS AND HONORS

2008	Shakespeare Competition Winner for the Hockaday School
2007	Best Young Actress of 2007 by the Observer Best of Dallas Issue
2007	Dallas Critics Forum Award for Best Actress for the Miracle Worker
2007	Cappie Nominee for Best Comedic Actress for Metamorphoses
2007	Best Actress nomination for The Secret Garden by The Column Awards

Your Head Shot

Your head shot should be exactly that, a picture of your face and shoulders. Some photographers like to take a three quarter picture that would show more of your body from waist up or from your thighs up. But for college auditions, I prefer a traditional head shot in color with a white border in a luster finish with your name centered at the bottom. I also recommend that you use a professional head shot photographer if your budget allows for it. Do not use a portrait photographer. Portrait photographers do not understand the correct and appropriate look for an acting head shot. They often will charge you exorbitant fees for the actual reproductions. Professional head shot photographers do not charge for prints. They will simply give you a CD of the shoot, a contact sheet, and a link to an online proof sheet. The printing of the actual head shot is something that you will take care of through a printer of your choice. Typically, printers are going to charge you a one-time set up fee of somewhere between $25 and $40. Subsequent eight-by-ten color photographic prints of your head shot should run in the neighborhood of $1 a piece.

 Be sure that your head shot is pleasant and welcoming and looks like you. You might decide that you want a happy. smiling straightforward head shot and something a little more thoughtful and pensive. Lisa Dalton's *Head shotology* is an interesting and worthwhile read if you want more detailed information about different looks and how to achieve the most from your photo shoot. Note that her advice is geared toward the professional working actor more so than high schools students looking to get into a college theater program. I include her info under "Resources."

Most head shot photographers allow you to do from one to five looks. A look is a change of clothes and maybe a slight alteration in hair and makeup or change in location or lighting. Here are two examples of what I believe are excellent head shots for college auditions. You can't see color here, but both are wearing bright solid colors:

My photographer of choice is Kelsey Edwards. Kelsey is based in Los Angeles but travels throughout the country to various cities and locations. I think there is no one better than Kelsey to capture your look and personality. She understands all the latest trends and has a caring, warm, and loving staff and stylist that will put you at ease. There is just no one better in my opinion. Kelsey will also help you with wardrobe choices and she understands how to capture your essence and your marketability. I give you Kelsey's information in "Resources."

Plan to print about fifty head shots and resumes. That should be enough for all your college auditions so that all the auditors have their own copy. That way you will have some extra ones if you have auditions the next summer or in the following year. These head shots should be up-to-date and a current representation of what you look like, assuming that you do not make any drastic changes in your appearance. An excellent head shot is an important investment because it serves as your calling card every time you have an audition. If you do not have the money to have professional head shots taken, you can certainly use your senior pictures from your high school. They will do just fine.

Your Wardrobe

The wardrobe choice for your audition and head shot is a reflection of your personality and marketable type. Your wardrobe—just like your monologues, songs, head shot, and resume—needs to be carefully thought out and coordinated so that you send a consistent and solid message to the auditors about how they can cast you. I recommend that your clothes be simple. Think J. Crew, Banana Republic, the Gap, and Old Navy. Wear solid colors that compliment your skin tone. Avoid patterns, stripes, and prints because they are distracting. These rules are true for everyone although I have made some exceptions for certain types of actors. For example, I had a student, a character actor, who regularly wore a multicolored argyle sweater vest and glasses. It seemed appropriate for him to wear an argyle sweater vest for his college auditions. This was very much who he was and how I was marketing him. Rather than a distraction from his performance, it underscored who he was. However, that was an exception.

In general, stay away from any bold patterns and just go with solid colors. And when I say color, I do not mean brown or black or gray; I mean colors that look good with your hair color and your skin tone and your eyes. Also, you need to think about clothes that fit you well and show off your figure and are not going to wrinkle. You will be traveling to a lot of auditions and sitting and waiting for long periods. Shop for clothes in a fabric that is going to stay fresh. It is important when you walk in the room for the audition that you look polished and crisp and not wrinkled and worn. Also, think about fabric that will be easy to wash and hang up in your hotel bathroom. Usually a knit or jersey fabric is a good idea.

For girls, I prefer a dress or a skirt and blouse. The auditors do want to see your figure. But you could certainly wear slacks if you would feel more comfortable or if the blocking in your monologue would prohibit you from wearing a skirt or a dress. I feel very strongly that legs should be covered for the audition. I know it is stylish now to go with bare legs. But for an audition I think it is completely inappropriate. Your legs should be covered with nude stockings, sheer black hose, black opaque hose, leggings, tights, or some kind of leg covering that will complement the rest of your outfit. I suggest that girls wear a ballet flat because most girls who are seniors in high school are not very experienced at walking in heels. On the day of your audition, you certainly want to wear a comfortable shoe. However, if you do want a heel and feel like you can handle it gracefully, I think it is perfectly acceptable to wear a low heel, but I would not wear a very high heel. I recommend a heel in the neighborhood of two inches. Your shoes need to be as simple as your outfit. A plain black closed-toe pump is always a good investment, and you could wear it for many auditions to come. If you already own a pair of character shoes and do not feel you can buy a new pair of shoes, then I think your character shoes are fine.

Refrain from wearing any jewelry. A simple stud earring is probably all right for girls, but anything more than that can be distracting to the auditors. I want the auditors to watch your performance and not be fascinated by or interested in what you are wearing. You want to leave a general impression that you looked terrific. It is about fit, fabric, color, simplicity, and comfort.

Guys should wear a nice slack, khakis, or corduroys with a solid color shirt tucked in with a belt. You could wear a V-neck sweater in a solid color with a T-shirt or collared shirt underneath. You need to look as though you have put effort into what you are wearing. Your shoes should not be a tennis shoe but rather a loafer or a lace-up shoe or a nice leather walking shoe like a leather Merrell or Sperry Top-Sider in a dark color, nothing distracting. Stay away from the blue jean and

T-shirt look unless you are marketing yourself as a tough guy, scrapper, or hipster. Your clothes need to fit well, not too loose and baggy. You should look pressed, clean, and fresh when you walk into the room.

One very important note: Guys and girls, no perfumes or colognes. Leave your favorite fragrance at home. Be sure that your hair is neat and out of your face. In addition, it is not a bad idea to have a back-up dress or a back-up shirt just in case you spill something on it.

Dance Attire

If dance makes you the most nervous, just remember, the auditors want to see *you*. They are not looking for perfection. Relax and have fun with the combination. And remember to smile.

Women

1. Everything should fit to your body.

2. Wear either a leotard and jazz pants or a leotard and tights. No shorts or footless tights. These cut off the line of your leg. (Even though people wear them for class all the time, auditions are a different story.)

3. Pick leotards with cuts and colors that flatter you, not black. A colored leotard makes it easier for the auditors to see and remember you

4. Wear black tights and shoes or tan tights and shoes. Create a long leg line.

5. Wear soft shoes, either jazz or ballet.

6. Do not wear jewelry.

Men

1. Everything should fit to your body.

2. Wear black jazz pants and a tight-fitting T-shirt (black or a flattering color, not white, unless it is very white and very fitted and you are very buff) or leotard and tights.

3. Wear a dance belt (basically a jock strap for dance). Compression shorts will work also.

4. Wear black jazz or ballet shoes.

5. Do not wear jewelry.

Chapter 11

Mental Management

The Importance of a Mental Program

You must remember that this is a competition. As with every competitive environment, it is very important to have a mental program as you enter the audition season. Otherwise, you will simply be in reaction mode. Not good. Your mental program should include coping skills for staying positive and focused before, during, and after the audition.

My students and parents have found great reward in studying mental management as it is offered by Mental Management Systems. What is mental management? It was designed and founded by Olympic gold medalist Lanny Basham. It teaches how to stay positive during competition and not let distractions or your environment negatively affect your performance. Facilitator Heather Sumlin has tailored the principles of mental management specifically for actors and college auditions. She has attended the Unified Auditions and coaches via Skype, iChat, phone, and e-mail. Her contact information is included in "Resources."

Mental management gives you tools that will be helpful not only during the audition season but also into your professional career. Let's face it, you are always going to be auditioning.

Some of the mental management tools include the following:

- How to deal with your competition in a healthy way
- How to combat nerves
- How to create a positive mental imprint
- How to prevent negative self-talk
- How to be a supportive parent without being invasive

An important ritual that Heather promotes, and one that I particularly find valuable, is keeping a performance analysis journal. My students write in it immediately following their auditions and make note of all the things that went well in the audition. Also, you should write down the names of your auditors in your journal. This is a great way to keep track of those you wish to thank or send a follow-up note or e-mail to.

During the Audition

You will find actors who want to talk about their songs and monologues as they are waiting to audition. I strongly advise against doing that. I think it is best to keep your material well guarded and private. Your audition material is very valuable and was chosen specifically for you. In many cases you have paid a coach or instructor for expertise in finding appropriate material and have worked very hard to prepare. Why would you want to share with your competitor your most prized possession? So do not do it.

You will also likely hear other students discussing specific auditions and sharing impressions involving the audition process. My advice is to avoid getting caught up in this kind of extraneous talk. As you wait your turn, stay quiet and focused. Keep your concentration on your own audition. Mentally go over your monologue, your objectives and actions, your song, your interview. Visualize yourself in the audition room, and stay positive. Do not let others distract you from the task at hand.

I had two students silently waiting in the hallway outside a college audition room at Unifieds when they observed a group of auditionees talking loudly. They were discussing material choices, the personalities of the auditors, and what they thought of their chances for admission. After listening to this for a while, my two students quietly looked over at each other and mouthed my name as if to say, "You must be one of Mary Anna's students too because we are the only ones keeping our mouths shut." That story made me laugh because it really said it all.

After the Audition

You will not be given any feedback after your audition. You will probably never know what the auditors thought of your performance. Although it is interesting to contemplate, it is an exercise in futility to guess what the auditors thought. You will *never* know what they thought. Remember that theirs is a subjective judgment and no amount of analyzing will ever give you an answer to that most interesting question Did they like me? or Why did they not accept me? This will get easier to accept as you continue to audition. It takes some actors years to be able to put their auditions into perspective and go on with their lives rather than waiting by the phone or constantly checking their e-mail. Two-time Tony Award nominee and University of Michigan graduate Gavin Creel was auditing one of our mock auditions, and I asked him about his mental attitude regarding auditions. He said that he always tries to have something else to do right after his auditions. He plans something to look forward to, coffee with a good friend or a project he is working on or just some errands to run. That way he is reminded that whatever the outcome, he has a personal life beyond the audition. It helps put it in perspective and serves as a healthy distraction.

Handling Rejections

Because of the highly competitive nature of the college audition process and the subjective quality of the decision, it is likely that you will get more rejections than acceptances. Coping with rejection is a natural part of the audition process. I think it is a very good idea for parents and students to discuss how to handle rejections. I send this e-mail to parents each year on the subject of acceptances and rejections.

It is important for you to discuss with your son or daughter how the news will be handled. Most notifications will come via snail mail, but some will be e-mails. Please come to an agreement with your child about how you wish to share this information. The letters will likely come while the student is in school. Will you text them? Call them? If it's a big envelope will you put it on their bed? If it's a small letter will you open it for them and then call them? Will you leave it all alone and let them open all the college mail?

As a parent, I am sympathetic. As a coach, I have seen that the best solutions involve mutual respect. Recognize that each child is different. Honor their feelings and agree on a plan that works for you and your child. Remember, MOST of the letters will be rejections. This can be a difficult time for your entire family. Please handle it respectfully and discuss this now.

I had a student years ago whose mother chose to hide all the rejection letters from her. The poor child never knew any results. As other's were finding out their college decisions, she was left in the dark, wondering. This sent a damaging message to the child of "you can't handle this". Please avoid any confusion and hurt feelings by discussing in advance how you wish to handle rejections as well as acceptances when they come in. Even acceptances need to be handled sensitively and thoughtfully.

Chapter 12

Acceptances and Rejections

This book is subtitled "The Ultimate College *Audition* Guide "because my expertise is in the area of the audition. The academic evaluation as it applies to college admissions is not my area of expertise. Although academic acceptance is obviously important, especially for schools with dual admission, I am not addressing it here. That information needs to come from a bona fide college counselor.

Acceptances

Schools with rolling admission will offer acceptances usually two or three weeks after your audition. Schools without rolling admissions will notify you of their decision in March or April.

Most acceptances will come via snail mail. However, some schools send initial e-mails, and some of the smaller programs like to make personal phone calls to deliver the good news. Most often they will call you directly on your cell phone. A complete acceptance package will eventually arrive in the mail. Information on financial aid packages may be included in the initial mailing, but some scholarship awards may arrive in subsequent mailings. Each school is different.

Rejections

Formal rejections almost always come in the form of snail mail. These form letters are cordial and brief. You will not receive any specific reason for the rejection or any audition feedback. I know of some specific occasions where a more personal e-mail was sent, but that is unusual and entirely up to the discretion of the theater admissions personnel and individual auditors.

Deferrals and Waitlists

Deferrals and waitlist notifications usually come in the form of e-mails and letters. A deferral means that a college is deferring its decision until all (or some portion) of the auditions are over. So the college has neither rejected nor accepted you but is placing you in the pool of applicants under consideration.

A waitlist means that a decision was made not to initially accept you. However, remaining on the waitlist gives you the opportunity to be accepted later if the school chooses to go to its waitlist if it does not fill all its slots with first-round offers. Some waitlists are ranked. Some are by type. Some are divided by male and female. It depends on the school.

One important piece of advice: If you are waitlisted or deferred by a school that you have a strong interest in, be sure you stay in touch with the appropriate people there regularly. Show that you are interested by updating them on any performances, improved test scores, awards, and honors you might receive. Or just send them a thank-you note. This would also be an excellent time to visit the campus.

Accepting an Offer

The national "reply-by" date is May 1. Any offer made to you stands until you have responded by May 1. A request in writing for an extension may be granted if you need additional time to decide. Schools would certainly like to get an answer from you as soon as possible after the offer is made (especially if they have rolling admissions), but you are not obligated to do so. You have until May 1 to make you final decision, except in the rare case when the particular department requires an earlier response. And I stress to my students, as a courtesy to others, please notify a school immediately if you have decided not to attend.

Students Bill of Rights (from the National Association for College Admission Counseling)

When You Are Offered Admission:

You have the right to wait to respond to an offer of admission and/ or financial aid until May 1. Colleges that request commitments to offers of admission and/or financial assistance prior to May 1, must clearly offer you the opportunity to request (in writing) an extension until May 1. They must grant you this extension and your request may not jeopardize your status for admission and/or financial aid. (This right does not apply to candidates admitted under an early decision program.)

If You Are Placed on a Waitlist or Alternate List:

The letter that notifies you of that placement should provide a history that describes the number of students on the waitlist, the number offered admission, and the availability of financial aid and housing. Colleges may require neither a deposit nor a written commitment as a condition of remaining on a waitlist. Colleges are expected to notify you of the resolution of your waitlist status by August 1 at the latest.

After You Receive Your Admission Decisions:

You must notify each college or university that accepts you whether you are accepting or rejecting its offer. You should make these notifications as soon as you have made a final decision as to the college that you wish to attend, but no later than May 1. It is understood that May 1 will be the postmark date. You may confirm your intention to enroll and, if required, submit a deposit to only one college or university. The exception to this arises if you are put on a waitlist by a college or university and are later admitted to that institution. You may accept the offer and send a deposit. However, you must immediately notify a college or university at which you previously indicated your intention to enroll. If you are accepted under an early decision plan, you must promptly withdraw the applications submitted to other colleges and universities and make no additional applications. If you are an early decision candidate and are seeking financial aid, you need not withdraw other applications until you have received notification about financial aid. If you think that your rights have been denied, you should contact the college or university immediately to request additional information or the extension of a reply date. In addition, you should ask your counselor to notify the president of the state or regional affiliate of the National Association for College Admission Counseling.

Chapter 13

Reauditioning

If things do not go as planned, you can always reaudition for college programs. It is done more often than you might think. Every year I coach a handful of new students who had disappointing results the year before and are trying the audition circuit again, this time with coaching. These students are another year older, wiser, and more mature in their preparations. Most important, they do not have the extra burden of being in their graduating year of high school. I often joke with these "repeat offenders" that senior year in high school is the last time a student and parent should have to go through this laborious and stressful process. When you consider reauditioning, there are two different ways to go about it.

Gap Year

You may hear the term *gap year* when discussing the reaudition process. Taking a gap year means that after you graduate from high school, you take a year off from formal school: community college, junior college, Most kids taking a gap year continue to live at home and possibly take a part-time job. They take the year to reevaluate their plan for college, research more schools, and better prepare themselves for another attempt at the college audition process. They still apply to colleges as a freshmen, and it has been my experience that colleges see this as a plus. The gap-year student brings a maturity that is a welcomed addition to the freshman class.

Most gap-year kids fill their days with private instruction in dance, voice, piano, or acting. They devote the entire year to a calm and steady preparation for their reaudition with private coaching. The reaudition kids whom I have coached always get very different and very positive results the second time around.

Transfer

Another way to reaudition is to take a year off after graduation and continue on to a community college, junior college, or university as a freshman liberal arts major while reevaluating your goals. You can get some general education courses out of the way and plan to apply to college as a sophomore or junior transfer when you reaudition. Be aware that admission will be more difficult as a transfer than if you were to take a gap year. That is because the odds are that there are fewer slots available in the sophomore and junior classes.

Some colleges with rigorous BFA programs will make you start as a freshman anyway. But in that case, your plans for getting general education credits out of the way might be considered a waste of time and money. Colleges that offer BAs might or might not take your credits. Important note: Even if you take one hour of any kind of college level course after having graduated from high school, you will be considered a transfer.

When I consult with a student who plans on reauditioning, it is always important to know where that student fell short and to diagnose the problem so that the same mistakes are not repeated the second time around. Most often it is a case of a "not smart" college list or ill-suited material. Another common cause is lack of proper mental preparation.

The Comeback Kid

I want to share this very special story with those of you who are considering reauditioning so that you know there is hope.

A repeat offender came to me in New York in the middle of the summer. He had found me through a former student. I met with him and his mother for a consultation. They were both distraught from his college audition experience. He had been the big cheese in his high school drama department in Iowa and had not anticipated the level of competition he encountered when he arrived at Unifieds in Chicago. He auditioned for only three schools and was accepted by one. He visited the one school that accepted him but did not see himself being happy there. So he reluctantly enrolled at the University of Iowa as a full-time student studying science. His parents were beginning to doubt his future career as a performer.

As I auditioned him during our consultation, I was very impressed with his talent and marketability, and his determination. I comforted both him and his mother and assured them that with my coaching they would be happy with his audition results. However, he had to do everything I asked of him. He seemed willing and eager to comply, and I felt certain I had the complete support of his mother as well. So we decided to move forward. We embarked on a steady, consistent eight months of coaching. These are his results for programs in musical theater.

Accepted
- Penn State University
- New York University
- University of Oklahoma
- Pace University
- Carnegie Mellon University

Deferred

- University of Michigan

He now attends his dream school, Carnegie Mellon.

I give you this example as an illustration that reauditioning is an option worth considering. In fact, it might just be the smartest thing you could do.

Conclusion

A BA, BFA, or BM degree in acting or musical theater is a solid undergraduate college degree that you can use for any number of pursuits, not just performing. You may ultimately decide on a career in a related field, such as a talent agent, theater critic, company manager, producer, or teacher. Many many adults are gainfully employed in a field other than the one noted on their college diploma.

If a career in any area of the performing arts is your passion, do not let anything stand in your way. Stay the course, and pursue the best training possible. As my Aunt Anne used to say, "Darling, don't *ever* give up until you get what you want!"

I hope this book is a helpful guide as you follow your dream and has introduced you to ways you can expand your world of knowledge about the college audition process.

If you are interested in coaching, let me hear from you. I have coaching studios in New York, Los Angeles, Dallas, Pittsburgh, Kansas City, and Atlanta. Please visit my Web site at www.collegeauditioncoach.com.

Break a leg!

Audition Tips from College Auditors

Acting is about bringing yourself to the work, about being confident in yourself, and about allowing others to see you as you are.

—*Dr. John Stefano, chairman, Department of Theater and Dance, Otterbein College*

Less Is More

An audition is not the time to try on extreme characterizations. We really want to see the person. People who come in and really reveal something authentic about themselves really stand out.

—*Lora Zane, professor of acting and directing, University of Southern California*

I admire them being risk takers, but I still don't know what they can do. Show me what you can do. I know what you *want* to do but what can you *really* do?

—*Arthur Bartow, former artistic director of NYU/ Tisch Department of Drama*

Show your thumbprint, show what you are. Leave accents at the door. Find material that is age specific. Be prepared and have additional material ready.

—*Tommy Newton, director of recruitment, Meadows School of the Arts, Southern Methodists University*

Be Yourself

I want to see you. I want to see your soul, your skill, I want to see you be a wonderful human being that I can connect with, that I want to be with for four years.

—*Amy Rogers, director of musical theater, Pace University*

We want to see you. We want to see if you are comfortable with yourself. Choose material that showcases you and your personality. Keep it simple. I'm not looking for a kid who is completely polished.

—*Kirsten Osbun-Manley, codirector Musical Theater Program,*
Ohio Northern University

We are looking to see the things that make you feel special and extraordinary in the world. Show us who you are as a person and as an artist. Keep it simple and honest. Have joy in your work and be brave.

—*Kaitlin Hopkins, director of musical theater,*
Texas State University

Show Potential

We ask, is there a product there that we believe will have some place in the industry? We are looking for raw product with a lot of talent, determination, and drive who can make a contribution to the industry.

—*Tom Orr, director of the school of drama,*
University of Oklahoma

Pick material that you have a strong connection with. Be cautious of picking material that is way outside of the standard rep. The auditioners will spend their time trying to figure out where they have heard it and not listening to your audition.

—*Raymond Sage, musical theater voice faculty,*
Pennsylvania State University

You don't need to come into the auditions as a professional since we are not looking for finished products. We look for people who we feel have the potential to be molded into professional performers.

—*Mark Madama, associate professor of musical theater,*
University of Michigan

Be Connected

I need to see if an actor is connected to the lines they are saying, if they have depth. I am looking for physical life, spontaneity, intelligence, and for a student who I believe will be flexible and open to our training.

—*Barbara Mackenzie-Wood, Head of Acting/Musical Theatre,*
Carnegie Mellon School of Drama

We want to see your passion for this art form. How do you personalize your material? How does the story of the song speak through you?

—*Victoria Bussert, head of musical theater,*
Baldwin-Wallace College

Choose pieces that you feel passionately about. We're hoping to see you reveal yourself through your work, not just show off what you can do.

—*James Crawford, assistant professor of theater,*
Southern Methodist University

Be Prepared

Do your homework. Find the colleges and theater programs that suit you. Research the curriculum, the faculty, the genres and styles of theater they produced, the opportunities to perform, the opportunities for internships and professional contacts.

—*David Mold, associate professor of theater arts,*
director of theater admissions, Marymount Manhattan

Give particular attention to the immediate moment before you speak your monologue or song, based on the given circumstances of the play. Your imagination is a powerful resource. Use it to create the impulse that brings you into the immediate moment of the monologue or song.

—Rick Walters, chairman, Theatre Department,
Viterbo University

Good preparation, choosing a piece that fits you well and *looking like you want to be there* will put you in the top 10 percent of people auditioning.

—Karen Kohlhaas, senior teacher, Atlantic Acting School,
NYU/Tisch School of the Arts

Be Smart

Please, please, please do age-appropriate material. Your youth, vitality, energy and passion are your strongest selling points.

—Aubrey Berg, chair of musical theatre,
Cincinnati Conservatory of Music

Truly understand the audition piece. Passion and artistry manifest themselves through an understanding of the work. Let that be your guide.

—Ken Martin, chair, department of theatre,
Coastal Carolina University

What will always win the day is being thoroughly prepared and doing work that is a truthful, genuine and real reflection of your life experience.

—Kent Gash, director, New Studio On Broadway, NYU

Resources

National Association for College Admission Counseling
Performing arts college fair
www.nacacnet.org

Schools for Theatre
Search for colleges by major
www.schoolsfortheatre.com

College Confidential
Web site with chat rooms
www.collegeconfidential.com

Susan Taub
Independent college counselor
susant@college-wise.com

Erin Ogren
Independent college counselor
www.cccollegeconsultants.com

Facebook
Social network
www.facebook.com

New Dramatists
Source for new playwrights
www.newdramatists.org

Karen Kohlhaas
Monologue advice for auditions
www.monologueaudition.com

National Foundation for the Advancement of the Arts
Source for monologues
www.youngarts.org

The National Unified Auditions
Regional auditions
www.unifiedauditions.com

Kelsey Edwards
Professional head shot photographer
www.kelseyedwardsphoto.com

Headshotology
Head shot advice from Lisa Dalton
www.chekov.net

The Drama Book Shop
Bookstore for plays
www.dramabookshop.com

American Theater Magazine
Magazine about all things theater
www.tcg.org

Playbill
Performing arts trade publication
www.playbill.com

Dramatics Magazine
High school drama magazine
www.edta.org

Mental Management
Techniques for staying positive during competition from
Heather Sumlin
heather@mentalmanagement.com

Summer Performing Arts Programs

These are a few suggested summer training programs. Included are those that my students and I have found valuable. Some require auditions and some do not. They vary in length and cost.

Camps

Broadway Artists Alliance, New York City, NY
Broadway Dreams Foundation, Atlanta and various cities
Broadway Theatre Project, Tampa, FL
Interlochen Arts Academy, Interlochen, MI
Stage Door Manor, Loch Sheldrake, NY
Stella Adler Studio, New York City, NY

Precollege

American Conservatory Theater, San Francisco, CA
Boston University, Boston, MA
CAP 21 Conservatory, New York City, NY
Carnegie Mellon Pre-College, Pittsburgh, PA
MPulse, University of Michigan, Ann Arbor, MI
Northwestern University Cherub Program, Chicago, IL
NYU/Tisch School of the Arts, New York City, NY
Oklahoma City University, Oklahoma City, OK
University of Southern California, Los Angeles, CA
University of California, Los Angeles, Los Angeles, CA

Study Abroad

The Oxford Experience, Oxford, England
British American Drama Academy, Oxford, England

List of Colleges Offering Degrees in Acting and Musical Theater

This is a comprehensive (though not complete) list of acting and musical theater degree programs. It includes BA, BFA, and BM offerings. Some require auditions and some do not. I have organized it by region. Your college counselor can help advise you on additional schools that may be appropriate, but this should be enough to get you started.

West

Arizona
Arizona State University
University Of Arizona

California
California Institute for the Arts
California State University, Chico
California State University, Fullerton
Chapman College
Loyola Marymount University
Notre Dame de Namur University
Occidental College
Pepperdine University
Santa Clara University
University of California, Irvine
University of California, Los Angeles
University of Southern California

Colorado
Metropolitan State College of Denver
University of Colorado
University of Northern Colorado

Nevada
    University of Nevada, Las Vegas

New Mexico
    College of Santa Fe
    Santa Fe University of Art and Design

Oregon
    Southern Oregon University

Utah
    Brigham Young University
    University of Utah
    Weber State University

Washington
    University of Puget Sound
    Cornish College
    Central Washington University

Wyoming
    Casper College
    University of Wyoming

Midwest

Illinois
    Colombia College
    DePaul University
    Illinois State University
    Illinois Wesleyan University
    Millikin University
    North Central College
    Northwestern University
    Rockford College
    Roosevelt University
    Southern Illinois University

University of Illinois Chicago
Western Illinois University

Indiana

Ball State University
Indiana University
Vincennes University
University of Evansville

Iowa

Drake University

Kansas

Friends University
Wichita State University
University of Kansas

Michigan

Central Michigan University
Oakland University
University of Michigan
Wayne State University
Western Michigan University

Minnesota

University of Minnesota, Duluth
University of Minnesota, Guthrie Theater

Missouri

Avila University
Kansas City University
Missouri State University
Missouri Valley College
Southwest Missouri State University
Stephens College
University of Missouri
Webster University

Nebraska
Creighton University
Nebraska Wesleyan University University of Nebraska
University of Nebraska at Kearney

Ohio
Ashland University
Baldwin-Wallace College
Kent State University
Marietta College
Ohio Northern University
Otterbein College
University of Akron
University of Cincinnati, Conservatory of Music
Youngstown State University
Wright State University
Bowling Green State
Heidelberg University

Wisconsin
Carthage College
Stevens Point University
University of Wisconsin, Green Bay
University of Wisconsin
Viterbo University

South

Alabama
Auburn University
Birmingham-Southern College
University of Alabama
University of Southern Alabama

Arkansas
    Ouachita Baptist University
Florida
    Florida State University
    Jacksonville University
    Palm Beach Atlantic University
    New World School of the Arts
    Rollins College
    University of Central Florida
    University of Florida
    University of Miami
    University of Tampa
    University of West Florida
Georgia
    Brenau University
    Shorter College
    Valdosta University
    Young Harris College
Kentucky
    Northern Kentucky University
    Western Kentucky University
Louisiana
    Louisiana State University
    Tulane university
Mississippi
    University of Mississippi
North Carolina
    Catawba College
    East Carolina University
    Elon University
    Lees-McCrae College
    Mars-Hill College

Meredith College
North Carolina School of the Arts
University of North Carolina Chapel Hill
University of North Carolina Pembroke
Western Carolina University

Oklahoma

Oklahoma City University
University of Central Oklahoma
University of Oklahoma
University of Tulsa

South Carolina

Coastal Carolina University
Coker College

Tennessee

Belmont University

Texas

Abilene Christian University
Baylor University
Sam Houston State University
Southern Methodist University
Southwestern University
Saint Edwards University
Texas Christian University
Texas State University
Trinity University
University of Houston
University of Texas at Arlington
University of Texas at El Paso
University of North Texas
West Texas A&M University

Virginia
>   James Madison University
>   Shenandoah Conservatory
>   Christopher Newport University
>   Emory and Henry College

West Virginia
>   West Virginia Wesleyan College

Northeast

Connecticut
>   Connecticut College
>   Hartford Conservatory
>   University of Hartford, The Hartt School

District of Colombia
>   American University
>   Catholic University
>   Howard University

Maine
>   University of Southern Maine

Maryland
>   Goucher College
>   McDaniel College

Massachusetts
>   Boston College
>   Boston Conservatory
>   Boston University
>   Brandeis University
>   Dean College
>   Emerson College
>   Northeastern University

New Hampshire
Plymouth State University
University of New Hampshire

New Jersey
Montclair State University
Rutgers University
Westminster College of the Arts at Rider University

New York
Adelphi University
Bard College
Fordham University
Hofstra University
Ithaca College
Long Island University
Marymount Manhattan College
Nazareth College
New York University, Tisch School of the Arts
Sarah Lawrence College
New York University, Steinhardt School of Education
Juilliard School
Pace University
Russell Sage College with NYSTI
State University of New York, Buffalo
State University of New York, Courtland
State University of New York, Fredonia
State University of New York, Geneseo
State University of New York, New Paltz
Syracuse University
University of Buffalo
Vassar College
Wagner College
Manhattanville College

Pennsylvania

Carnegie Mellon University

DeSales University

Marywood University

Muhlenberg College

Pennsylvania State University

Point Park University

Seton Hill University

Susquehanna University

Temple University

University of the Arts

West Chester University

Wilkes University

Rhode Island

Rhode Island College

University of Rhode Island

Vermont

Bennington College

Johnson State College

Middlebury College